your
LION
INSIDE

Tapping into the
Power Within

KIMBERLY FAITH

Your Lion Inside
Tapping Into The Power Within

Copyright © 2017 by Kimberly Faith

Published and distributed by KF Enterprises, Inc.

The characters and all stories in this book are real people. The names and identifying details such as individual circumstances, occupations, physical attributes, and geographical indicators have been changed to protect the privacy of individuals.

www.KimberlyFaith.com

Faith, Kimberly

Your Lion Inside: Tapping Into the Power Within/ Kimberly Faith

Pages cm

1. Women executives 2. Leadership in women. 3. Self-Help

Digital ISBN: 978-0-9990501-0-1

Editor: Kat Walsh

Interior Design: Hannah Nichols

Cover Design: Jun Ares

2nd edition, March 2018

Dedicated to Susan B., Rose Agnes, Linda Diann, Linda Sherrill, Heather Marie, my daughters, nieces, granddaughters, great granddaughters, and all of my #sweetsisters around the globe . . .

As our past, present, and future intersects,

may our PASSION be timeless,

our LOVE everlasting,

and H.O.P.E. prevail.

May we have FAITH in each other and in ourselves.

 Contents

A Gift for You

The reality is that we have an enemy far greater than any regime, any organizational intent, any unconscious bias, any principle designed to keep us in our place. There was a time when we had to battle the collective because the culture was overpowering.

The collective was, and sometimes still is, wrong. And in many places around the world, the battle for the rights of women is still going on – as it should. But while we are looking at that foe, another is trying to sneak in.

Slowly. In stealth mode. Insidious. Quiet, yet so pervasive many don't see it.

Blinded to reality much like a fish is to water.

I saw it and want you to see it too.

As long as we believe the answer is ***out there*** - above us, below us, beside us - we will never fully embrace the real source of our power.

> *Each morning when you look in the mirror*
> *~ in the reflection ~*
> *IS the answer you seek.*

This collection of wisdom serves as a light in the darkness. A manual of truth. A balm for the battered soul who knows, deep down, there is so much more. Driven by a deep-seated desire to BE more – DO more – GIVE more.

Therein lies the paradox.

You are already enough. More than enough.

Together, let us remove the dust that has dimmed the treasure and gently begin polishing what is underneath - for you and the whole world to see.

I am enough and so are you,

Kim

Breaking Free

"We can't take a bag of change here, lady!" the clerk said gruffly and loudly. The seven people behind me in line waiting to check out all stared at me. *All I want to do is buy three gallons of gas so I can see my daughter,* I wanted to scream. Instead, I turned and ran out of the store, clutching my bag of change with tears streaming down my face. It was June of 2008 and gas had skyrocketed to over $4.00 a gallon. I dumped the change onto the seat of my car, pulled out the quarters and went back in to purchase one gallon of gas. I wanted to see my daughter before she left for school.

In our few precious minutes together, my daughter's happiness filled me with the fuel I needed to last another day. After saying goodbye, I drove to the storage building where everything I owned was stuffed into a 10 x 10 unit. While searching for a change of clothes, I stumbled and fell. Rage, blame and fear claimed what little sanity I had left. I remember sitting on the floor, back up against the wall, looking out at the clear blue sky and asking myself, "How did I get here?"

The day progressively got worse – calls from one debt collector after another, voicemails with threats from an investor relationship gone terribly wrong. I was separated from the husband at the time, and we were alternating months as to who would live in the house with our daughter Heather. It was my turn to live away only, I had nowhere to go. I had no money in my checking account, no credit card that worked and the start-up I had so passionately launched was crashing around me. All I had was that damn bag of change.

I remember vividly coming to terms with the fact that things were so messed up the world would be better without me. I was driving down Interstate 85 alongside a section of cement medians and it hit me that with a simple flick of a wrist, it could be over. The pain could end. The temptation was *so strong* . . . just think of all the problems it would solve! The million-dollar life insurance policy would take care of everyone who was losing money . . .I would not be able to make any more wrong decisions . . .everyone would heal and move on. I was a failure anyway, so what value could I possibly have left? I knew I was close to making an irreversible decision.

Emotionally, I crossed a dangerous line that night. In the darkness and tears, I had a flashback to something I used to teach in systems thinking. *Structures drive behavior* I would tell audiences. Right then I made a rule – a structure – that I would never ride on the highway again at night. And I didn't for nine months while I fought to save the company my daughter and I started called Sassytails.

I don't know when it happened . . .I don't know *how* it happened . . .but somewhere along the way, I decided I didn't want my story to end that way. I made a conscious choice to teach my daughter *how to fail with grace.*

That dark time in my life forced me to re-evaluate everything I once knew and believed.

Despite the darkness, I discovered a powerful path to freedom.

A freedom which can take life to new heights.

This manifesto of hope can take you there too.

Time is an Illusion

The afternoon of Wednesday, March 7, began in a remarkably mundane manner. On the way home, I stopped to vacuum my car. When I inserted my first quarter into the slot, it wouldn't fit. *Broken again?* I thought. But no, my quarters were too big. How did that happen? I looked closer – in my hand were several Susan B. Anthony coins. *Haven't seen those in a while,* I thought. I dug up the required quarters and went about my mundane day.

Reading the news the next morning, I saw that it was International Women's Day. As my husband and I headed out to meet his daughters Alicia and Abby for breakfast, I had a thought. *I should give those Susan B. Anthony coins to our granddaughters in celebration of the day.*

But first, some googling. I needed to refresh my knowledge on the achievements of Susan B. Anthony so I'd be able to explain them in a way that would make sense to a curious 7-year-old.

At breakfast, my 3-year-old granddaughter, Rowen, silently accepted her coins with a hug and a smile. My 7-year-old Ava, as predicted, was full of questions. "Why did she have to fight to vote?" "Haven't women always had the right to vote?" I had to explain to her that her great grandmother Rose was born *before* women had the right to vote. She was SO surprised - she could not comprehend there was ever a time when women could not vote.

11

Once I explained it, she said, "Thank goodness for Susan B. and all of her friends!"

On the drive home, I thought about the journey of the past 100 years and great grandmother Rose, my 101-year-old Italian mother-in-law. Born February 22, 1916, a decade after Susan B. Anthony passed away, my mother-in-law was four when the 19th Amendment was ratified on August 18, 1920.

A momentous occasion in women's history - a history that was staring me in the face, figuratively and literally. Susan B. Anthony, in spirit, and Rose Agnes, in the living room asleep. Day by day, as history and the future collided in the here and now, the purpose of this book was becoming clearer.

And that was the end of Susan B. Anthony and me.

Or so I thought.

Later that afternoon, I was desperate for a break from writing the first draft of this book. For some reason, a certain book called out to me, *The Great Work of Your Life* by Stephen Cope. I'd started reading it months ago, and then, well, life got in the way. But the book's message – to live your truth or sacred duty, your dharma - had encouraged me before. I guess I was searching for further inspiration.

I read about how Jane Goodall, Henry David Thoreau, and Robert Frost lived their dharma. All very inspirational and thought provoking. Then, in chapter six, I saw an eerily familiar name. Susan B. Anthony.

I almost dropped the book!

So, Ms. Anthony and I meet again. All within a 24-hour period and on International Women's Day, no less. Obviously, Susan B. Anthony had something to teach me – and my granddaughters.

I was ready to listen. Recently, in working on this book, I had hit an internal wall. Deep down, I knew I had an important message to share with the world, but still, I was struggling with self-doubt. *What right did I have to live LARGE and shout to the world the wisdom I know as truth? Why am I living small, like a kitten, when I have the strength of a lion trapped inside?*

Unfortunately, I know I am not alone in these struggles. I've been asked these same questions thousands of times after training a roomful of incredibly talented professional women.

Why are *they* living so small when they have so much to offer the world? Why are *they* introducing themselves in a way that does NOT own the value they bring to the table?

Why is it so difficult for us all to accept a mere compliment, much less fully embrace the gifts *we* have to offer the world?

Susan B. Anthony did indeed have a message that day.

The same sentence that described her life - "No great character in American history has been more ill-served by stereotyping, lame biographies, and stuffy hagiography" - also describes women who pursue leadership positions today. One hundred years later, and here we are, fighting the same fight.

Did you know that Susan B. Anthony would not be content to be a "good enough" public speaker? She had to be great and she became single-minded in her practice. She found a coach in her closest friend, Elizabeth Cady Stanton. Everything - the way she dressed, the way she took care of herself, even the way she spoke - was re-examined. She poured her heart into doing whatever it took to become the powerful person she knew she MUST be to make a difference.

Her passion fueled her when the world would not.

Clarina Howard Nichols, another women's rights advocate, wrote to Susan, "It is most invigorating to watch the development of a woman in the work for humanity:

- first, anxious for the cause and depressed with a sense of her own inability;
- next, partial success of timid efforts creating a hope;
- next, a faith;
- and then the fruition of complete self-devotion. Such will be your history."

Such will be your history, I whispered over and over again.

And then came the sentence that in my eyes changed Susan B. Anthony from a teacher to a sister: "Susan B. Anthony was determined not only to act on behalf of women, but to mobilize women to act for themselves."

There it was, THAT was the reason I was writing this book. The. Exact. Same. Reason. **TO MOBILIZE WOMEN TO ACT FOR THEMSELVES.**

Touched at my core, I was overwhelmed with gratitude for this sister from our past. We hear you, sweet sister. We hear you.

It was 9:47 p.m. on March 8, 2017, the evening of International Women's Day.

AWARENESS IS THE FIRST STEP

Your conscious mind has been telling you one story
but your unconscious mind is <u>writing</u> a different one.

Awareness is the first step when it comes to *seeing* the world differently. When we are in "it," it is like swimming in a fishbowl. We don't realize the ones beside us are also in the fishbowl because we are all in the water, looking out. I believe the same thing is happening to women: we are in the fishbowl with a narrative - one that is blinding us to our personal power - and we don't even know it.

Awareness plucks you out of the fishbowl, shakes you off and sets you down next to it, allowing you to see clearly for the first time. When your perspective changes, everything begins to shift.

Every single disruption we see happening today is because someone chose to step outside of a "fishbowl" to see things differently. An internal choice was made *first* to see things differently. The #MeToo movement is one example of what happens when women jump out of the fishbowl, see the Narrative for what it really is and disrupt it. And it is only the beginning.

This book is about jumping out of the <u>fishbowl</u>. The time has come to disrupt your own self.

The Glass Ceiling Is Also a Mirror

Once upon a time (in 2018), a newly married couple was in their kitchen, enjoying each other's company as they prepared pot roast for dinner. The husband watched his wife cut off both ends of the pot roast before seasoning it and placing it in the oven. He thought it odd – he'd never seen anyone in his family do that. "Honey, why did you cut off both ends of the pot roast?"

She paused briefly and said, "I'm not sure. My mother always did."

At the next family gathering, the husband approached his mother-in-law. He explained what his lovely wife did and then asked why she cut the ends off the pot roast. His mother-in-law paused—briefly—and said, "My mother always did." The mystery continued.

Weeks later, the family gathered to visit their grandmother at the retirement community she now calls home. The newlywed couple could not help but approach the grandmother, 100 years old, born in 1917. They explained the scenario and asked why she cut off the ends of the pot roast. The grandmother looked at her daughter and granddaughter. "Because my pan was too small!" she said.

Subsequent generations behaved a certain way because of the information they absorbed from observation. No big discussions. It was not written down as part of the recipe. It simply happened in the busyness of life. The unwritten rules snapped into place. The original problem—a too-small pan—was no longer an issue.

Here we are in 2018. A world away from 1918. Or are we?

REWRITING THE NARRATIVE

Unlike Susan B. Anthony, we live in a society where many (not all by far) people value women and actually want us at the table. We live in the era of Sheryl Sandberg's *Lean In*. Like many, I was thrilled when *Lean In: Women, Work and the Will to Lead* was published. It was exhilarating and empowering to see a woman with such influence change the conversation from what women can't do to what we can do. It was 2013, and I'd been working with numerous women's groups on many issues Ms. Sandberg had addressed. The national dialogue that followed was invigorating, passionate, and fueled a movement in much need of re-energizing.

But then, the pushback began. The collective conversation escalated into a debate about the role women played in leaning in vs. the role organizations had in breaking the glass ceiling. The pendulum swung from empowering women to blaming the culture, the companies, the good ole boys, and "the system." It reached a fevered pitch when, for the first time in history, a woman was a major party's nominee for President of the United States. We watched live, in color, as the ugliness of the campaign spilled toxicity into the culture. As the results of the election became a reality, tears rolled down the faces of hundreds of thousands of women—young and old—who believed all hope was lost. The heartbreak was real.

The ongoing collective narrative—women must overcome challenges, women are held down by "the system," women must endure inaccurate perceptions—has run amok in the media. Daily, the headlines, tweets, editorials, and updates are reinforcing a mindset that I believe is now standing in our way. What is the mindset? It is our view of *the Narrative.*

The Narrative is the collective storyline we have been listening to since birth—we've heard it from our families, from society, and from the workplace – regardless of where we may live in the world. It has so infiltrated the culture that we have embraced these very distorted perceptions as truth—and nothing could be farther from the Truth. We might not be able to see it, but we sure can *feel* it. It's akin to a ton of bricks sitting on our shoulders, each one representing the boundaries drawn *for* us, the boxes created to *contain* us, and the beliefs suffocating our potential. It is as if every baby girl was given a book at birth on how to live life, already half-written *by someone else* with the unspoken expectation to simply "deal with it." **We have another choice.**

The #MeToo movement is a powerful testament to the choices we do have - a pivotal step on the journey ahead to dismantle the Narrative, brick by brick. Once the Narrative is brought to our attention, we begin to see it for what it really is. Then, and only then, can we consciously choose to close that half-written book and open a new one with beautiful, blank pages to create our reality. Only then will the truth of our potential—our story—come to light. Only then will we truly tap into the power within freeing the lion inside.

A new narrative is asking—begging—to be written. Who will write it? We will. I invite you to join me in authoring this new and necessary narrative. Humanity depends on it.

VICTIMHOOD, POWERLESSNESS AND JUST: THE MEAN GIRLS OF YOUR MINDSET

Victimhood. She was someone I knew all too well, but I had to say goodbye to her years ago. Victimhood seems like a friend at first, shifting your focus from what **you** need to do to what everyone else has done **to you**. It is comforting to have someone take your problems away, to give you a break from your own reality. That escapism is the lure of social media, our devices, and reality television. It is also the foundation for addictions to food, alcohol, and drugs.

Much like other debilitating distractions, Victimhood can be mesmerizing. Empty promises of addressing the pain right now, **today**.

If they would do this or that, Victimhood whispers. *Others need to do their part.* At first, hanging out with Victimhood seems to be helping, until you meet her other friends. Powerlessness—nicknamed *"I can't!"*—is Victimhood's best friend. Powerlessness rears her ugly head when Victimhood begins to lose her luster. Drama, friend to both, waits in the shadows to stake her claim too.

"What do you mean you are tired?" Victimhood demands. *"Stay the course . . . they OWE you."*

Powerlessness chimes in, *"How dare they do these things to you. How dare they ask so much of you!"*

"Don't they know YOU are the victim here?" Victimhood says.

"Just keep doing what you are doing," a new voice appears. It's Just, perhaps the most dangerous girl of the group, for she can explain away anything.

If they could JUST . . .

I was JUST trying to . . .

I would be successful if they would JUST . . .

If they would JUST remove the barriers . . .

If they would JUST stop judging me by their standards . . .

I could earn more if I JUST had a chance . . .

If they could JUST see how *their* bias is standing in our way. . .

THE POWER IGNITES WITHIN FIRST

I know there are larger societal issues that play a big role in the way women are treated, from the bedroom to the boardroom to the big screen. Yes, we absolutely must slay the dragon of disrespect every time it rears its head. However, after many, many years spent coaching women, I have found that if our focus remains external, if we are always looking at what others are doing *to us*, we miss countless opportunities *for us*. The real power comes when we look within. Once you shift your focus internally, you will find that you CAN change YOUR life.

Much like the energy of an atom, which creates everything, you also have the power to create. Create a new life, a new movement, a new reality for yourself and for others. Once the power is ignited within, it cannot be contained. The power to shift the direction for the next generation lies inside each one of us. As we consciously shift our focus, this new perspective has the potential to create a tsunami of change. One woman— one sister—at a time.

Seeing through the Narrative and embracing powerful mind-sets for our own life *first* is the key that will unlock the collective shift we desire. When we change what we see in the mirror each day and the inner dialogue we have with ourselves, the collective power to create a world that truly values women will emerge. The answer does not lie outside of ourselves. Therein lies the paradox. Every time we pause, reflect, and consciously choose our direction, we create a new reality—individually and collectively.

WHICH PATH WILL WE CHOOSE?

As women, we are at a crossroads, a critical intersection between what was and what will be. We are facing an unprecedented window of opportunity this very moment. An epicenter of great change. An invisible threshold of sorts. We have two choices: victimhood or victory. We can take the path well traveled right now and buy into the Narrative that more people are *against* us than *for* us. We can choose to focus on negative statistics like the pay gap. After all, rarely does a week go by without the Narrative reminding us that men make more than women. We can accept the notion that many seem to view our inherently female characteristics as a negative. We can buy into the Narrative's emphasis on inequity. Multiple workplace reports acknowledge how "inequities are taking a toll on women." And why wouldn't they? The sheer thought of tackling the beliefs that we are wronged in *so many* ways feels daunting. It leads many to feel powerless and look "out there" for reasons why they're not succeeding to the level they're capable of. If we believe we are powerless, our language and our actions will reflect it—often unconsciously. You will see this issue come to light throughout this book.

Some of the messages in the headlines today appear to be conflicting. We read about women in technology and their struggles for equality in Silicon Valley. Then we hear that in 2017, the number of female CEOs jumped by 50% to 32, the most women ever to make the Fortune 500 since the list started in 1955. Or do you even recall hearing that statistic this year? Recently, *Time* magazine launched its impressive multimedia project, Firsts, spotlighting the successes of women who have broken into a field. All of these are tap dancing on the Narrative. The momentum of the #MeToo movement and subsequent naming of The Silence Breakers as the 2017 Person of the Year is offering us all an unexpected opportunity to reassess what we have accepted as *normal*. The time has come to redefine what normal should be.

For women, individually and collectively, the question becomes: which story is going to take root: victimhood or victory? Powerless or powerful? Will we choose to shift our focus to the power we DO have or will the Narrative, with all of its negative perceptions that we (and our neurological pathways) have grown up with and grown accustomed to, continue to take a front row seat?

As a professional speaker and coach for C-level executives, I see the thirst for inspiring messages in women of all races and ages, across all levels of corporate leadership, spanning the globe. Recently, I had a conversation with a wildly talented, ambitious professional, a young woman in the defense industry. The topic of our conversation: where could she find a female role model? Every single week, women around the world ask the same question. Where are our female role models for leadership?

However, there's a potential problem hidden in that question. As women, are we looking for a role model or are we searching for a hero? Do we want someone to lead us or save us? Even today it surprises me the number of people, at all levels of an organization, who are still looking for a hero. So many look up for the answer, down for the answer, to the right and to the left for the answer. Yet the answer lies within. You *are* the hero you seek.

We will never shatter the glass ceiling until **each one of us owns our piece of the Narrative**.

Day by day. Decision by decision.

What does owning our piece of the Narrative mean?

- It means not accepting every headline as fact and instead testing it on your own terms.

- It means looking inward for the power to change your future.

- It means being able to articulate your value authentically and fearlessly.

- It means you don't wait for anyone to give you permission to live to your fullest potential.

- It means not making excuses for why you are being held back.

- It means digging deep to uncover the subconscious roadblocks standing in your way.

Here is where the real power lies: choosing to focus on individual change as much, or more in some instances, than collective change.

HOW WE THINK ABOUT CHANGE

"Women early in their career are the least likely to <u>believe</u> they have equal opportunities for growth and development."

-2016 Lean In Women in Workplace report pg. 10

"Young women are . . . significantly <u>less confident</u> they can reach the top of the organization."

-2017 Lean In Women in Workplace <u>report</u> pg. 19

On September 27, 2016, Sheryl Sandberg wrote an article for *The Wall Street Journal* discussing the findings of the *2016 Women in the Workplace* <u>report</u>. The report, Ms. Sandberg said, found that women who hit the glass ceiling early, are far less likely than men to be promoted from entry level to manager, and hold less than 30% of the roles in senior management. The 2017 report echoed many of the same findings.

Why is that?

The book you are holding in your hands explains why. Why are many women not making that early jump in their careers? And why do they lose ground the more senior they become? This time, it is not about "them." It is about our misperceptions that distort what we see in the mirror every day. *Has the time come for us to consider that the glass ceiling is also a mirror?* By this, I mean that it is time for us to look at ourselves in the mirror and see that there are specific beliefs, assumptions, and mindsets standing in our way. These mindsets don't show up in the new workplace surveys because women themselves don't even realize that the mindsets are standing in the way. Why? It is unconscious and the Narrative has convinced them otherwise.

I am on a quest to inspire women to realize we have more power than we think we do. May a global, collective conversation be ignited so that we are all more **aware**—for ourselves, for each other, and most importantly, for future generations.

For my sisters who have little interest in data or limited patience for the background of the premise of this book, I invite you to jump ahead to the section titled **Corporations Can't Do It Alone** *on page 41. Many of your sisters require this insight in order to move forward. Both approaches are valid, just different.*

The following explanation is based on a US perspective but could be mapped out using multiple global examples *in light of when <u>each country</u> granted women the right to vote - see page 266 for a list. The key learning is the thought process and the power of unintended consequences.*

The fight Susan B. and so many others dedicated their lives to began in the mid-1800s and lasted for over fifty years. During that time, the only way they were able to change the culture was through collective change. Take a look—

However, progress does not move along in a simple, linear fashion. There are always unintended consequences—sometimes positive, sometimes negative. Being aware of these unintended consequences invites us to take a second look so we don't become trapped in shifting the burden unconsciously. Take a look—

In 2020, the United States will celebrate the 100th anniversary of women earning the right to vote. My 102-year-old mother-in-law Rose lived with my husband and me for two years. Daily, as we cared for her, I was reminded of how long—and how short—one hundred years really is. So much has changed during her lifetime - and some things have stayed the same.

A centenarian, whose parents emigrated from Sicily to Massachusetts in the early 1900s, sees the world very differently. Rose's curiosity and wit remain as sharp as ever—throughout the day she listens to the radio, wanting to know the state of current affairs. When the Women's March took place in January of 2018, she was baffled that so many women all over the world felt the need to march. After all, women were much better off in 2018 than they were in 1918. "We all had to work hard in them days, regardless of how women were viewed," she said. "Why don't women today just focus on what they can do to better their situation? We never had time to march. There was too much to do!"

Here is how Rose—and many others—see the fight for equality.

But remember that part about unintended consequences?

COLLECTIVE VS. INDIVIDUAL CHANGE

Now what? This is beginning to sound like the age-old argument of what comes first: the chicken or the egg. In our case, it's what needs to come first: collective change or individual change?

Many women take for granted the freedoms they enjoy today, simply because they don't understand the significant battles previous generations fought to earn those freedoms. And yet, here we are, having some of the same conversations in 2018 that we had in 1918. Dissatisfaction with the status quo in the U.S. reached a tipping point on November 8, 2016, igniting and reviving the national women's movement. Attendance and participation in the Women's March and International Women's Day in 2018 crushed expectations. And recently, the juxtaposition of two art installations in the heart of New York City—Fearless Girl and Charging Bull—are reminders of the collective debate about the power of women.

Much of this was driven by one galvanizing moment: when the dream of the first female President of the United States did not become reality. Regardless of which side you were on, we now have a front row seat to a growing dilemma for women's empowerment. A crossroads between victimhood and victory. Between powerless and powerful.

Now, we read headlines such as "Breaking the Glass Ceiling Starts with Changing Workplace Culture" and coverage of Equal Pay Day in April 2017 is based on the premise that "If a woman makes 20% less than a man, she should pay 20% less for the purchases she makes."

Is it possible that we are pushing the system in the wrong direction?

Do we still need to come together collectively to drive the cultural change we want? YES! Collective change drives cultural change and cultural change drives even more collective change. Let the #MeToo movement of 2017 serve as a powerful reminder of the impact and importance of collective change.

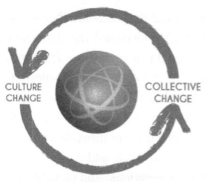

In one hundred years, our culture *has* changed; however, it hasn't changed *enough*. We can all agree on that, but can we agree on how to get where we really want to be? This much is certain: we can't keep using the same techniques that women used in the early 1900s. Yet it seems that some are using the same old playbook. If it worked once, it should work again, right? Wrong—the system has changed. Let me explain.

COLLECTIVE *AND* INDIVIDUAL CHANGE

Think of it like parenting. New parents follow a certain set of rules and use specific skills with their baby. As the baby becomes a toddler, parents change the rules and their approach. No one in their right mind would use the same parenting skills for a toddler and a teenager. Why? Because the two are entirely different. Ask any parent: raising a teenager is a very different experience than raising a toddler; it requires sharper parenting skills. Fortunately, it is 'easy' to adjust because the parent sees the child grow up. **The women's movement has grown up too.** It now requires additional insight and skills. Collective change is <u>not</u> the only tool in our toolkit. Individual change is a key factor. Take a look—

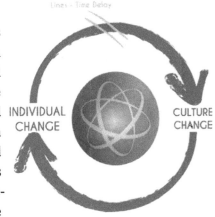

The same issue exists here as before. It takes a long time for individual change on its own to drive culture change. Cause and effect are far removed in space and time: we are still impacted by the mindsets from the generations before us *and* we have the power to impact future generations one hundred years from now.

It is important to truly grasp the *interdependence* of the actions of those who came before us and those who will come after us.

Recently, I had an eye opening, yet informative, conversation with a millennial woman, one of the many professionals I had asked for feedback on this book. "Why do you even mention Susan B. Anthony in the book?" she asked. "She's not relevant to today's world."

Wow. *Not relevant?* Even if this woman never cared to vote in her life, Susan B. Anthony made so much more possible for all of us. For me, her reaction was a startling reminder of the short-term focus most of us have. This 33-year-old woman was blinded by what she couldn't see, even though it was right in front of her. I realized that I needed to do a better job of connecting the dots.

If it were not for the actions of many brave and committed women like Susan B. Anthony over one hundred years ago, we might still be dealing with the issues they did. Can you imagine not being allowed to stay overnight in a hotel alone or speak in public without fear? Can you picture a life in which all your assets became your husband's when you married? And can you believe that those "assets" included your children? In comparison to *that* type of life, having conversations about shattering the glass ceiling would be a luxury.

Thankfully, because the women before us fought these obstacles, many of us (not all) live in a different world than they did. We are free to have the conversations we do—about gender differences, about the glass ceiling, about sexual harassment, about rewriting the Narrative. But conversations can only take us so far; we have reached a tipping point where collective change is not the only answer.

So, what is the answer?

Balance.

Both collective change **and** individual change are needed. Without the other to provide balance, the pendulum swings too far to one side. Think of this balance like a pair of glasses. If we had only one lens, what we see would be distorted. A clear image emerges ONLY when we look through both lenses.

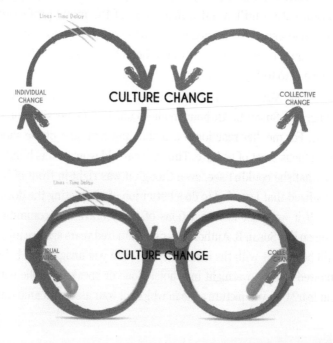

If we each buy into the current Narrative—that collective change is THE answer or it is simply the system that is broken—the unintended consequence will be decidedly negative: a mentality of victimhood. If we continue down this path, the outcome is predictable.

Let us be reminded of the power of a self-fulfilling prophecy. Most people believe the problem is "out there"—that if the other person would change, then everything would be okay. The self-fulfilling prophecy, however, shows otherwise. The power is in shifting OUR beliefs and assumptions first.

THE POWER OF PROPHECY

Here's one example of the power of a self-fulfilling prophecy. If a teacher believes a student is smart, that belief will influence the teacher's behavior toward the student. The teacher will spend more time with the student and offer more encouragement. Naturally, the student then believes *the teacher must think I am really smart.* This belief drives the student to work extra hard, thereby reinforcing the teacher's belief: this student is smart.

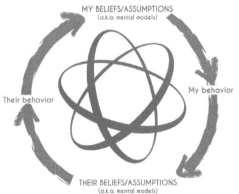

What happens if the teacher assumes the opposite?

If the teacher believes the student is not smart, that belief will also influence the teacher's behavior toward the student. The teacher would likely spend less time with the student and offer fewer words of encouragement. The student then believes, *the teacher must not think I am really smart—why should I even try?* This belief drives the student to not work hard, thereby reinforcing the teacher's belief: this student is not smart.

This is not an indictment of teachers; it is simply an example that's easy to understand. The same cycle could be explained with a spouse, parent, boss or anyone else in our world. We have all felt the effect of this in our lives, whether we realize it or not. The main takeaway is this: self-fulfilling prophecies can lead people into either a downward or upward spiral. Whether it goes in a positive direction or a negative direction is a direct result of our beliefs and assumptions.

Now, let's look at a different example: the narrative of women's empowerment. A woman walks into an interview. She believes the odds are stacked against her from the start. She has been told they usually hire men in this industry. She knows it is a long shot. And she just read an article about men making more than women. Already, she feels that she can't win. Despite her best intentions, her behavior reflects nervousness, a bit of fear, and maybe even a lack of confidence. She holds back from sharing all her accomplishments—that would be bragging. She assumes her resume speaks for itself. Her behaviors impact the judgment (a.k.a. assumptions) of her interviewers. She has the skills, but something is missing. *She is just not ready yet*, they assume. *She needs more executive presence*, they explain. As a result, the interviewers do not offer her the job, which reinforces her original belief: the odds are stacked against her.

Let's see how this situation plays out in a different culture with a different narrative. A woman walks into an interview. She just read a magazine article stating that women make $1.07 for every $1.00 men make. When researching the company she was interviewing with, she learned 54% of their leaders are women. In fact, she was friends with two of these women in college and always felt inspired by their success. She knows the workplace culture supports women through various stages of their life—there is even a daycare on site. She believes (a.k.a. assumes) she is a perfect fit for this company. Those beliefs translate into her walking into the interview with a spring in her step. She speaks confidently and manages the interview so she is in the driver's seat. She blows the interviewers away. *This woman is a go-getter,* they assume. *We need her on our team pronto!* They offer her the job. *I knew I was a perfect fit for this company,* she thinks.

Was it them or was it her?

I know, I know—we don't live in a world where women make $1.07 for every dollar men earn. We don't live in a world where company leadership is 54% female—*yet.* So yes, there is a significant gap between those two scenarios. This book is about bridging that gap.

HOW WE THINK AND FEEL ABOUT GENDER DIFFERENCES

One of the many professionals I spoke with researching this book was Dr. Matthew Price, a well-respected pioneer in media psychology and applied behavioral neuroscience and VP of Global Media & Technology for Nielsen Consumer Neuroscience. He thought I'd be interested in the emerging field of sentiment analysis, which, broadly speaking, uses artificial intelligence to determine the attitude of an audience with respect to a select topic.

When I told him I was very interested, Dr. Price introduced me to Centiment, a research company doing groundbreaking work in the field. Their program uses artificial intelligence to analyze over 1 million data points, including world news, global trends, and social media in real time, to calculate the emotions surrounding any topic. Micah Brown, Centiment's founder and CEO, took a few of the topics covered in this book—the glass ceiling, gender bias, women in the workplace, and gender equality—and ran a sentiment analysis on these topics.

The results, especially in the social media sphere, shed light on the worldwide impact of the Narrative. The general emotions surrounding these issues, in order of strength, were:

- Anger
- Disgust
- Sadness

Worldwide, the general vibe toward the topic of gender differences is **overwhelmingly** negative. Although the field of sentiment analytics is still in its infancy, these results offer compelling insight into not only the language women are using to discuss these issues, but also the *emotions* behind their words.

In addition to this sentiment data, when it comes to the current state of affairs, there are three cognitive biases at work here as well. The first is **the bandwagon effect:** the more people who hold a belief, the greater the probability that we will each adopt the belief. For an example of this, all we have to do is think about the conversations we have had or heard on the subject of women's empowerment.

Add to that the second bias at play here: **the availability heuristic.** With this bias, we tend to place too much value and importance on the information that is available to us. Each week a newspaper headline, a popular blog post or media interview is drawing us into the collective Narrative, albeit sometimes unconsciously.

The final bias at work is **anchoring,** the tendency to rely too heavily on the first piece of information offered when making decisions. *Is it possible that women, anchored by the constant, repetitive cultural and gender stereotypes they face daily, are unconsciously agreeing with the general belief that women are less capable in some way or that the challenges we face are insurmountable?*

Slowly but surely, the victimhood mentality is trying to take root. The Narrative looks and sounds more and more like victimhood. It is not easy to see at first glance.

Remember the parable of the boiled frog? If you put a frog in a pot of boiling water, it will immediately jump out because it senses immediate danger. However, if you put a frog in lukewarm water and slowly turn up the heat, it will boil to death because it does not sense the gradual, growing danger.

Are we in danger of being boiled?

Dr. Price believes it is quite possible: "I spend a lot of time studying the nature of reality and the human experience. I try to objectively explain how our worldviews and collective consciousness meld to become what we generally agree is reality. But our reality is nothing more than a social contract wherein each of us, men and women alike, agree to certain norms and expectations. To fulfill that contract, we have an unspoken responsibility to each other, to find in ourselves balance and equality; only then can we hope to expect the same from others."

This is powerful insight from a behavioral neuroscientist and media psychologist who specializes in interpreting the messages we collectively receive every day. The drumbeat of what we can't see is so loud we can no longer hear it.

LOOKING AT GENDER
DIFFERENCES DIFFERENTLY

Perhaps, in order to lead the Narrative away from victimhood and toward victory, we need to think about gender differences differently. Although by no means a comprehensive review of all the literature on these topics, three recent studies offer insight and advice. And while their findings may not be conclusive, they certainly are eye opening.

Downplay the Difference

A July 2017 Columbia Business School study focused on how the way women discuss gender can affect their workplace confidence and behavior. The conclusion: gender-blindness (the belief that gender differences should be downplayed) is a more adaptive strategy for increasing female workplace confidence than gender awareness (the belief that gender differences should be celebrated).

It appears that *decreasing* the focus on gender might be a more adaptive ideology for closing the confidence gap and helping women take action to shape their career outcomes.

Power and Gender Identification

In a study from July of 2016, professors at Yale and New York University examined how high-power mindsets affect gender identification. They found a direct link between holding power and lower group identification: women who were made to feel powerful reported lower levels of gender identification. Interestingly, this effect was not found in men.

Such results can help explain Carly Fiorina's response to becoming the first female CEO of Hewlett-Packard in 1999, "I was completely unprepared for the amount of attention that was paid to my gender . . . I had so long ago stopped thinking about myself as a woman in business, and thought about myself as a businessperson who happened to be a woman."

Hollywood Isn't Helping

A study published in *Organizational Dynamics* in 2013 reviewed over one hundred films featuring managerial and professional women in lead or support roles in order to identify specific biases in how such women are portrayed on film. Overwhelmingly, researchers found how the media does not "frame" women in positive or empowering ways. The portrayal of professional women is frequently represented as deeply flawed or wanting, while depictions of women's attempts to advance professionally are generally less than flattering.

In their conclusion, the researchers agree: "As we face the ongoing conundrum of the glass ceiling, the role of the media in perpetuating this problem deserves further exploration and critique. Films, along with commercials, television shows, and online content, communicate socio-cultural understandings that shape viewers' perceptions of reality, in particular their <u>mental models</u> of appropriate gender roles."

Talk about playing games with our subconscious! Given virtually unfettered access to 24-hour media channels, the media plays a pivotal role in the development of adolescents and adults. Young women are particularly vulnerable to internalizing media messages. Add to that the subtle messages sent through underrepresentation in corporate communications and the overwhelming number of headlines espousing the bias against women, we can begin to see how the Narrative came to life. **Is it possible that as women, we have unknowingly become partners in keeping the Narrative alive and well?** The entire storyline we have all bought into around the glass ceiling—which wasn't commonly used in our vocabulary until 1986 when *The Wall Street Journal* used the phrase —is a societal problem.

As of 2018, the women in Hollywood are trying to help. In response to the #MeToo allegations that upended (or ended) the careers of many powerful men in the entertainment industry, over 300 prominent actresses and female agents, writers, directors, producers and entertainment executives formed <u>Time's Up</u>, a movement dedicated to fighting systemic sexual harassment in Hollywood and in blue-collar workplaces nationwide. "They didn't come together because they wanted to whine, or complain, or tell a story or bemoan," said Maria Eitel, co-chairwoman of the Nike Foundation and a moderator of Time's Up meetings. "These women came together because they intended to act."

Remember, the studies above, and countless others, are all influenced by the Narrative tap dancing on the collective subconscious. It is helpful to think of the Narrative as a person—a living, breathing entity that draws strength from our need to seek heroes and place blame. Blinded by what we can't see, the Narrative is counting on our staying unaware. **What if** we consciously placed the Narrative to the side, and, shining a bright light on that which is lurking in the shadows, started a fresh blank page?

CORPORATIONS CAN'T DO IT ALONE

Regardless of numerous workplace reports, growing diversity initiatives, and increased awareness, the sobering reality is corporations can't do it alone. The mindsets fueling the Narrative are being absorbed—like the pot roast lesson—long before we enter the workplace. This is true for men and women. In our short-term driven world, let us pause long enough to understand that cause and effect is far removed in space in time. Take a look—

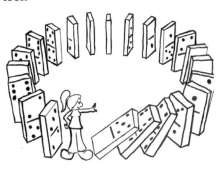

When we first push the <u>domino</u>, it takes a long time for the last domino to fall. Having a greater understanding of how the workplace is but one chapter in a much larger story is crucial to our ability to truly change culture. There are a multitude of unintended consequences to our inner dialogue as women, for ourselves, our children, and the young people we mentor. May we be brave as we consider the unspoken messages being passed down from generation to generation. May we boldly embrace our power within to rewrite a new reality.

WHAT HISTORY HAS TO TEACH US

I adore the movie *Hidden Figures,* the true story of three brilliant African-American women at NASA who were the brains behind one of the greatest operations in history: the launch of astronaut John Glenn into orbit. Here we see three women succeeding ***despite*** the limiting narrative at the time. How easy, how tempting it would have been for these women to become friends with Victimhood and Helplessness. But instead, Mary Jackson, Katherine Johnson, and Dorothy Vaughan crossed all gender, race, and professional lines to own their piece of the Narrative. And when they did, they forged a new path and broke the mold on what everyone else saw as possible.

They shattered the glass ceiling before "the glass ceiling" was even a thing. Their stunning achievement restored the nation's confidence, turned around the Space Race and galvanized the world. And their story—despite how long it took to be shared with the world—is a powerful testament to the message of this book.

Same goes for us today: We will never shatter the glass ceiling—or the bamboo ceiling—until **each one of us owns our piece of the Narrative**. It's our story, played out day by day, decision by decision.

What if Mary Jackson, Katherine Johnson, and Dorothy Vaughan had been friendly with Just?

What if Susan B. Anthony - and other activists like Ella Baker, Sojourner Truth, Alice Walker and many others - had been friends with Just? How different the world might be. But they weren't friends with Just, and you don't have to be either.

FROM MEAN GIRLS TO SWEET SISTERS

No one was more surprised than I to find a universal set of beliefs standing in our way that transcended age, race, culture, economic status, or leadership position. It had to be more complicated, didn't it? Sadly, that is a myth too many have bought into. There is great power in Simplicity. Become friends with her on this journey. Simplicity feels lighter, more inviting, and nobler. A true friend.

Earlier I introduced you to Victimhood, one of the Mean Girls who can inhabit your mind. Victimhood, you see, tried to befriend me quite early in life: I was born with a significant hearing loss. *You have a disability!* Victimhood whispered. Fortunately, I was also born an optimist, so instead of seeing a devastating disability, I found an inspiring teacher. To effectively manage everyday life, I learned how to assimilate much more than what people said. I listened to *what people didn't say.*

That ability led me to Truth, a brilliant personality who has since become a soulmate. On this journey called life, Truth has introduced me to Power, Strength, and Hope. They are quite a crew—endearing, fun, creative, and courageous. Together, they led me to the Sisterhood of Seven: Seven Stories, Seven Mindsets.

They are all standing by, arms open wide, with an invitation to rewrite the Narrative. The Sisterhood of Seven will introduce the most common beliefs unconsciously standing in our way and more importantly, it will show how to shift those beliefs so we each can tap into the power within.

It starts with you and me. Right here. Right now.

A Message From Kim

YourLionInside.com Video 1

The DNA of Thought:

More and more, we are looking to DNA for answers in life. We can gain insight into our lineage with a DNA Ancestry kit. We can map out our health and wellness with a DNA health kit. DNA forensics is changing the landscape of criminal justice. The potential of DNA to change the way we understand the world is in its infancy. Is it possible we are missing a profound connection to the figurative DNA embedded in our thoughts?

When searching for answers to what we cannot see, is it possible we can look to the DNA of our thoughts in the same way we look to the DNA of our body? I believe there is a great potential in understanding this perspective. Why am I so convinced it could be the key to a very different future for us all? Take a look as my dance with the Sisterhood continues . . .

My watershed moment happened in 2002. My daughter Heather was 5 years old. I was 100 pounds overweight. I read an article in a parenting magazine about how a parent's health was the biggest indicator of how healthy a child would be. Really? I had flashbacks to all the struggles I'd had with weight, with a significant eating disorder and the years of heartache of never feeling I was enough. I was unhappy with my personal life and trying to eat my way to happiness. While work was fulfilling, the demands caused significant hardships at home. I lived in a small town and some days felt like I was living my own version of *Groundhog Day*. I realized everything I was about – the good and the bad – was going to be passed down to my daughter.

Sobering, to say the least. Life changing, to say the best.

In that moment of insight, I committed to do whatever it took to change the course of *her life*. I did not want her to live through the constant pain I battled for decades. Like so many women, I could not muster up enough love *for myself* to make the changes needed; however, the love *for my daughter* provided a wellspring of strength. That love fueled me with determination and fortitude. In that galvanizing moment, everything changed – for me and for her.

It was at that crossroads when I came face to face with the generations of distorted thinking about women, about life, about self-worth that had been passed down to me. Can you relate? Each generation's outlook on life had grown more distorted due to life's hardships – almost like a misfiring in DNA sequencing.

I was dangerously close to passing along the previous generation's thinking to my daughter and send her down a predictable path of hardship—a path where Powerlessness and Victimhood ruled the day.

It started with counseling to discover the root of my bulimia. I had taught systems thinking for seven years by then, so I knew my own mental models blinded me. *I did not know what I did not know.* First, I had to face the demons that ran through the family line. The emotional abuse, alcoholism, the survival mindset and the limited value of women – all placed on center stage for my review. Forced to grow up in poverty on the streets of Connecticut, my father's worldview was impacted by having to fight his way through life – and by having an abusive father who eventually abandoned his family, leaving them to fend for themselves.

My mother was raised by a woman who was from a family of eight, working on a tobacco farm in North Carolina. Family was valued and there were good memories; however, survival was paramount to love – a pervasive undercurrent that permeated the lives of each child. My mother was 19 when she married my father. Each one came into the marriage with less than what they deeply needed growing up. Two people needing more than the other could provide, ending in a toxic divorce when I was thirteen years old.

Second, I had to consciously choose which mindsets I would release that were not healthy. This was an agonizing journey that brought me face to face with my responsibility for what I was willing to pass down to my daughter. I was the first in my family to obtain a four year college degree, which ultimately led me on a solid path out of "survival" mentality. Then came the loss of almost 100 pounds, changing my appearance; I even got a new car. What seemed to be a simple mid-life crisis was much more. It was a reclaiming of my identity. The changes on the outside were reflective of the significant metamorphosis inside.

I started to consciously choose to see the world through a different lens, asking many questions along the way. The good news is life started to shift. The bad news is I came face to face with the consequences of many choices I made before this new Kim awakened. Back when I was a distorted version of myself, it was an awkward place to be. It was sobering to realize generations of confused thinking had led me to where I found myself. I slowly realized my external life was no longer a reflection of who I was inside. I could feel significant shifts on every level: cellular, soulful, emotional, spiritual. The gap between who I knew I was deep down and the persona the world knew as "Kim" was widening. The more it widened, the deeper I felt myself sinking into the mess.

I was in a crazy house, some of my own making, like a big messy ball of twine all wound up. Powerless and Hopeless were my constant companions. I unknowingly placed myself into a cage for over a decade genuinely believing there was no hope.

Time passed.

Each year, I tried something new, doing the best that I could with what I felt life "dealt" me. It was surprising to discover there was more to the sisters than I had thought.

When I was 30, a decision was made for me: my lifelong dream of having lots of children was not going to happen. It completely devastated me. My heart splintered into a million pieces - the heartbreak was overwhelming. That decision was the final nail in the coffin of the marriage; although it would take another thirteen years to hold the funeral. The desperation in the meantime almost drowned me. Yet the beautiful daughter I *was* given kept me afloat and inspired me to keep searching for the best version of myself.

The leverage for us as women? *We love others more than we love ourselves*. It is the unspoken epidemic of our time. When we become conscious of it, that epidemic can become our silent superpower.

The Toolkit

Many of us are not inclined to change until we feel pain. It could be the pain of not feeling well or poor diagnostic results that drive us to change our eating habits. Perhaps it is the pain of enduring a difficult marriage. Or maybe it is the pain of not receiving the job or that promotion you worked so hard for. Whatever the situation, pain is often the catalyst for change.

Why is it, though, that one person can face a painful situation and break free, yet another person stays trapped? Why can one woman face a divorce and go on to create a new life full of joy, while another woman's divorce becomes the defining moment of her life and keeps her spinning in a downward spiral? How is it that one woman who loses a spouse is able to move through the pain and end up finding joy again, while another allows the pain to become her story with no hope for happiness? The difference in these women and their reactions is *perspective*. And it's the gift pain gives us. Take a look:

*P*ath to

*A*nother way;

*I*nvitation for a

*N*ew direction.

On the journey through life, the toughest parts are the intersections. There is always a choice: *will I be a victim or the victor?* Think of all the stories that have inspired you. If you listen closely, there's always talk about choosing a different path. They don't talk about casually meandering through life and suddenly, "Oh! I got lucky – things turned out differently. Yeah me!" Most inspiring stories also do not mention a hero swooping in to save the day. Instead, they focus on digging deep to discover the reservoir of strength that lies within. Whether the pain is collective (the struggle for women's empowerment) or individual (how will I feed my family?), the power lies in change being an inside job FIRST. When we shift what we think on the inside, everything else will slowly begin to change. The hope for change lies in each one of us learning how to **H**arness **O**ur **P**ower Everyday.

THE KEY TO TRANSFORMATION: YOUR MINDSET

After training and coaching tens of thousands of leaders, I learned that the key to transformational change is shifting your individual mindset. These leaders would invest their energy in learning new skills, trying different techniques and giving themselves a daily pep talk to overcome their fears and failures. These efforts would help, but not in a dramatic way or for very long.

Why? Because inevitably, the deeply held mindsets and beliefs of these leaders would bubble up, unconsciously at times, and mitigate any progress made. It was a bit like waxing a dirty car: the shiny new polish won't last long if a problematic foundation is still underneath.

To truly understand the power of an individual's mindset (including your own), it's helpful to look at the concept of mental models. Mental models are the lenses through which we see the world. They're the specific set of glasses we wear. They're not right or wrong, they simply are. We have mental models about everything: the way kids should be raised, the way the company should be run, the way governments should be led or how we should age.

Have you ever met someone who is "old" long before his or her time? Somewhere along the way, this individual was told that his birthday was not a good thing because it meant he was getting old. Hence, this person hates birthdays and everything else that comes with age. Look for ailments to pop up as this person slows down because he has convinced himself he is old. I don't know about you, but years ago I chose a very different approach to aging. I decided I would be like fine wine and get better with age!

The discovery of America is another example. At the time, in the early 1400s, the prevailing mindset (a.k.a. mental model) was that the world was flat. Along comes Christopher Columbus's discovery of America in 1492 and voilá, a new mental model was born: the world is round. Did the world change shape? No. What did change was what people believed.

The danger of mental models is that we are often *unconsciously* operating from them. We don't even realize they are influencing our decisions. Mental models are often like blinders on a horse: we see only what they allow us to see. In fact, mental models drive the entire notion of confirmation bias, which is the tendency to search for, interpret and recall information in a way that confirms our existing beliefs. Even if we are surrounded by facts showing us other ways, we stick with what we already know, in effect, blinded to any other option (or opportunities).

MY OWN MORNING MENTAL MODEL

Here's a personal example. Part of my morning routine at home is to make a piece of toast for breakfast: I take out a slice of bread and stick it in the toaster. While it's cooking, I set out the jelly, knife and a paper towel. Toast pops up, I make my breakfast and go on with my day. One week, after dealing with a lot of travel mishaps, I returned home very late, practically dragging myself into the house. Morning arrived.

"I'm going to make toast," I said to my new husband. Five minutes later, he walked into the kitchen and saw me reading the paper.

"Honey, where is your toast?"

"I couldn't make toast this morning," I said, pointing to the empty roll on the holder.

Silently, my husband walked over to the cabinet, grabbed a new roll of paper towels and put it into the holder. He then watched me, in my tired stupor, stand up and go about making my toast. Later, we had a good laugh about it, but this is a great example of how a mental model can *blind* us to other options.

Let's dissect what happened:

I had a habit of putting toast on a paper towel. Past experience had taught me that toast makes a lot of crumbs. I'd tried various options, but selected the paper towel option because it caught crumbs and made clean up fast and easy. And for a decade, this was the way I "viewed" toast making. To someone on the outside, it was glaringly obvious there were other options: I could have used a small plate, big plate, no plate, etc. However, my mental model – my deep unconscious thought pattern – blinded me to all those other options. In effect, I was paralyzed from pursuing other options.

I will never forget hearing a veteran speak after me at a conference for Dell Computers in Austin. *Four days* before his tour of duty ended, the enemy captured him. He spoke of the struggles of spending four years of his life trapped in an 8x8 foot cell. Imagine how he felt when he was released and was free again.

Even though I heard him speak twenty years ago, I clearly remember his words, "After I returned, it was an adjustment to fit back into the real world again. Years passed and I actually became grateful for that experience. One of the most startling realizations for me when I returned is that every day, I saw people who were far more trapped by the eight-inch square in their heads than I ever was in that POW cell."

Powerful and true - I see it happen to leaders every single week. They are so entrenched in their world – trapped in that eight-inch cage inside their heads – that they can no longer see clearly. Even worse, *they don't even know they can't see clearly.* This is one reason why it so important for legacy companies who have been around for a long time to bring in new talent. It offers perspective. Mental models are extremely powerful. Do *not* underestimate them.

THE POWER OF MENTAL MODELS

Mental models can even influence entire companies to not see the world changing around them. Busy seeing only what they want to see, these companies miss critical signs. Back in the 1990s, I did quite a bit of training with Kodak, whose headquarters were in Rochester, NY. Every other month, I would train their leaders. I became very familiar with the Kodak mindset and saw how many thought alike. It was a subject we discussed often because there was a growing concern that the longevity of most of Kodak's leaders was impacting the company's ability to grow into new markets. Think back for a moment. What was the prevailing mental model about photography at the time? It was film. Pictures are forever, right? At the same time I was training Kodak, I watched Fuji move their North American headquarters to my small South Carolina town, building miles and miles of space to manufacture film. Fuji's prevailing mental model was also film. Two global brands were both planning on things staying the same.

We all know what happened to the photography industry: it went digital. And a new mental model completely transformed the photography industry. Do you know who invented digital photography? An engineer at Kodak. In 1975. So the obvious question becomes, why didn't Kodak lead the way in a new digital revolution? The answer: the leadership could not *see* the potential of digital; they were too focused on other things. I was sharing this story with aerospace leaders when a leader, who used to work for Kodak, stood up in the back of the room.

"I remember those days," he said. "All of us at Kodak were too busy focusing on one-time use cameras. We were building manufacturing plants all over the world to meet the demand. When the idea of digital came up, we were too busy doing other things. We completely missed the shift. I watched my beloved company go from 65,000 employees down to 2,500."

There are many stories of industries missing the changing world around them because they were blinded by their own vision, missing huge opportunities in the process. In the 1980s Sony, the market leader at the time, completely missed the industry shift from hardware (i.e., Walkmans) to software. The mental models of Sony were blinders to seeing new possibilities. However, Apple did see the shift coming. The company gave us the iPod and the digital music industry (let alone Sony) has never been the same.

Another example: Blockbuster and Netflix. Did you know Blockbuster's CEO had a chance to buy Netflix in the early days? However, Blockbuster's leadership could not "see" the future demand for video streaming. It has been called one of the biggest misses in the boardroom.

As we enter an age of accelerated change, we have a front row seat to the same kind of radical disruption across multiple industries. New mental models that have the potential to significantly shift how we see the world are unfolding rapidly. Whether it is the ongoing disruption of the transportation industry by companies like Uber or the predicted adoption of self-driving cars, our future will be very different. Artificial intelligence and augmented reality are poised to revolutionize our world in ways we don't yet fully understand. Cryptocurrency, and the blockchain technology behind it, has the power to transform global economies and financial markets. In each instance, the adoption curve will be impacted by our ability to shift mental models and embrace change. Time will tell who will be the next Kodak or Blockbuster.

That is the power of mental models.

THE DANCE OF CHANGE

Now that you can see how mental models can be blinding, the question becomes, how do you change what is standing in your way?

It takes three steps.

STEP 1. PAUSE

Remember my toast story? It takes conscious effort to **pause** long enough to catch the automatic thought process and shift it in a different direction. But between every action and reaction, there is a **space** and in that space is the opportunity for change. It is your Pivot Zone - it's where we pause long enough to stop ourselves from the automatic reaction. In that space we find *awareness*.

ACTION   PIVOT ZONE   REACTION

STEP 2. REFLECT

Once we pause and catch that automatic thought, we then have to ask why. Why did I say that? Why did I do that? Do I really believe that **or** did someone/something else influence me? Am I reacting consciously or unconsciously? What is it that I am not saying out loud?

The theory is if you ask why seven times, you will eventually find the truth. You will likely discover that something happened in your past that your mind took a snapshot of. You unconsciously placed that snapshot into your mental folder called *This Is The Way Things Are*. Without knowing it, you have been placing things in that folder for your entire life. You collected some items from your family - many from your mother, others from your father. You added a few things from teachers and bosses.

Any time something out of the ordinary happened, you placed it in a different folder titled *Never Allow This To Happen Again*. Much like a file cabinet, these mental folders eventually reach a point where they're overflowing with stuff. The thing about our mental file cabinet is, we rarely pause long enough to ask which files should stay and which ones should go. We simply keep filing stuff until our brain is overflowing with mindsets (a.k.a. mental models) that have outgrown their usefulness. The system grows up – *like a teenager* – but our mindsets stay the same – *like a toddler*.

The Sisterhood is saying, *"Ladies, it is time to clean out the files. There are too many beliefs which are now standing in the way, individually and collectively."*

STEP 3. CHOOSE

We have the power to choose. We really do, although that power is often buried under a lot of shoulds, don'ts and can'ts – all that the world has stuffed into our mental folders. The Sisterhood wants to wipe away all that has blinded us from possibility. It is important to remember that small actions have BIG impact. The changes the Sisterhood is asking from us will happen day by day, decision by decision. It is not one HUGE shift –its hundreds of small shifts taking place each day to each of us that will eventually creating a tsunami of change in the way we think and live.

HOW TO SEE –AND DO – THINGS
DIFFERENTLY

Anytime we go on a journey, it is helpful to know what's ahead. Before you meet the Sisterhood, there are three things to remember:

First, there is a reason you are reading this book. Something triggered you to buy it or someone passed it along. Either way, these things don't happen by accident. Know there is a nugget of treasure for you buried in the following pages.

Second, make a conscious choice not to allow doubt, the busyness of life or even fear to stand in the way of this journey. Don't be surprised if there is a time or two you feel uncomfortable while reading - accept it as a signal you are knocking on the door of a personal breakthrough. Simply breathe deeply and keep reading. The message meant for you will reveal itself soon enough. Don't run away; choose to be brave and good things will happen.

Lastly, *trust the process.* Our process here is much like looking at a picture on your phone: you can see the big picture in its entirety and you can also zoom in to focus on one area in detail. We will do the same thing here. In the first chapter, the journey began with the big picture - on the mountaintop, taking a collective look at the whole. Now, we are zooming in to look at the smaller parts. At the end, we will zoom back out to see the big picture again. Remember, trust the process.

A Message From Kim

YourLionInside.com Video 2

Meet the Sisterhood

You just read about the power of mental models. But before you can change mental models, it's helpful to know *exactly* what is standing in your way. What do those mental models *look* like in your daily life? What do they *sound* like in your thoughts and words?

It is time for you to meet the Sisterhood.

Each of the seven sisters represents a mental model, hidden deep down inside each of us, that is unconsciously influencing our actions. At first glance, some of these mental models may seem obvious. Others may sound shocking. To be honest, I was surprised to see some of them myself. My first reaction was disbelief: *No way. We have come too far! We can't still be thinking this way.* But then, I did my own research. I started testing each mental model, one by one, with the thousands of women I've worked with around the world, across industries, race, ages and backgrounds; across cultures, leadership positions and experience. And my results consistently led me to one conclusion: like it or not, the Sisterhood is right.

The Sisterhood has a story to tell. And it's one every woman needs to hear.

THE SISTERHOOD SPEAKS

Before you learn about the mindsets of each sister, you want to meet them and get to know them a little, right? I felt the same.

So here they are – all seven of them – gathered around a long, loud and lovely family table: Kari, Ranee, Gabriella, Darsha, Avalene, Jalila and Nikki.

NIKKI: Since you were a child, you have been learning how to navigate the life into which you were born. Depending on where and how you were raised and your life experiences, we will speak to you differently.

AVALENE: Each of us has a message; however, you will relate to two or three of us best. Worry not, though. The seasons of life are such that you will run into each of us as you need to, and you will come to know and learn from us all.

DARSHA: Some of you might think these mindsets are too obvious. But trust me, if they really were that obvious, there'd be no reason for this book. Or us.

KARI: Trust us. We know. It breaks our heart every time we see the light within you dim a bit more with each passing day.

JALILA: We are here to show you *how* these mindsets manifest in your life. So keep an open mind as you hear our stories and the lessons we have learned.

AVALENE: Think of it like a decoder for a treasure map. Except this time the treasure is you - in your fullness. Peaceful, strong, comfortable in your own skin with a healthy love of self that radiates to all those you touch.

GABRIELLA: The best thing you can do for your family is to learn how to be your best self. And the best thing you can do for your employees is to lead from the best version of yourself.

NIKKI: But girls, the point is that the best way to be of service to humanity is to live from your core. Be exactly who you were meant to be – YOU. No less, no more. When that happens, even you will be shocked at the amount of time you have spent on pain and stumbling blocks needlessly.

The sisters all nod in agreement.

RANEE: Here's the thing. We want you to see the Sisterhood as a bridge to *freedom*. Freedom from the self-sabotaging behaviors standing in your way. Freedom from the limitations the world has placed on you. Freedom from the limitations you place on yourself.

DARSHA: And freedom from all of the expectations weighing you down. Those expectations are like tin cans clanking behind your car – loud and unnecessary! I am telling you, it *is* possible to free yourself from these things. It is. It is. It is.

KARI: So you might be wondering, why exactly is this a sisterhood? It's because the mindsets we represent are very, very familiar to us all. You already know them quite well. So well, in fact, that they are like family.

DARSHA: And like family, you know us at our best. You've lived with us at our worst.

GABRIELLA: Sisters can be best friends. Always available to talk to and count on. Even when we haven't seen each other in awhile, a simple "hey" is all it takes to start the conversation again.

RANEE: Sisters can also be tough to manage at times. We each have a different perspective and see the world so differently.

AVALENE: The best part is that a sisterhood loves each other. Unconditional love holds us close, no matter which side of a sister shows up. It is our foundation, a special language only we can understand.

DARSHA: We protect each other, no matter what. Even when a sister is acting all, you know . . .

KARI: Crazy and stuff? Yes, even then. *Especially* then. Sometimes it is in our craziness that we need our sisters the most.

JALILA: Even when we are frustrated and having a hard time accepting brutal honesty. Even when we fight and disagree, *especially* then, we protect one another.

RANEE: For me, the best part of the Sisterhood is that we all agree on who *not* to let in.

DARSHA: That's for sure! We don't let in Just, Victimhood or Powerlessness.

NIKKI: But that doesn't stop them from showing up. All three of 'em still occasionally come knocking at the door.

GABRIELLA: Same thing with Fear. We won't let her in, we can't, but I am telling you, that girl shows up wearing fangs! And if you let those fangs sink in, it literally will suck the life right out of you.

AVALENE: That's true. And when she does show up, I always remember who she really is: False Evidence Appearing Real.

RANEE: Judgment is definitely not welcome here either, although she *always* tries to sneak in, attempting to convince us that it is less painful to stay trapped in a troubling mindset than it is to do the work and shift out of it.

GABRIELLA: Yep. Judgment and all her mean little friends are terrified of what would happen if everyone in the sisterhood tapped into the power within.

DARSHA: Don't let Judgment, Fear, Victimhood, Powerlessness or Just fool you. They are all black-belt ninjas at perpetuating the Narrative that the rest of us are working so hard to dismantle.

JALILA: And even worse? If you happen to accidentally let even one of them in, they will sabotage each of us, each of our mindsets, every single time.

KARI: That's why we never let them in – they serve no one and will do nothing to move you forward. For every single mindset you will read about, know that there was a valid reason for it *at the time.* Maybe it was to keep peace in the family. Perhaps it was to fit into the group, at school, church, a specific organization or the office.

AVALENE: Or the mindset was forced upon you and you had no choice.

KARI: Whatever the reason, you needed the mindset at the time. Okay, so it happened; release it in loving kindness and compassion. Forgive yourself and others. Know this journey is to uncover what is unconsciously operating as truth in your world and find out if it still serves you today.

JALILA: It's quite possible you are carrying mindsets that arc no longer needed. If a mindset doesn't serve you, you can replace it with a new one. We'll show you how. But if a mindset is serving you, keep it.

NIKKI: Remember, this process is about *consciously* making choices. When you are conscious, you are aware.

KARI: I'm sure we could go on forever, but I'll wrap it up for now by saying we are honored to have you join us on this journey. We've been wondering when you would finally see us. Welcome to the Sisterhood.

CHANGE IS A CONTINUUM

All of the mindsets are part of who we are. There is no letting judgment in, remember? We simply want to use the mindsets that inspire us to go forward more often.

To avoid the inevitable judgment that comes with polarized declarations - good versus bad, right versus wrong - the mindsets of the Sisterhood are explained using a traffic light as an analogy.

We begin by looking at the mindsets standing in our way. These are the hidden belief systems that influence our behavior – and we don't even realize it. Our goal is to stop allowing these mindsets to stand in our way. Take a look and see if any of the following sound familiar:

As each sister reveals herself to you, it is important to remember that change takes place on a

THE KARI STORY
KARI — I expect perfection

THE RANEE STORY
RANEE — I have to meet all demands

THE GABRIELLA STORY
GABRIELLA — I need permission/approval

THE DARSHA STORY
DARSHA — I should accept what is said

THE AVALENE STORY
AVALENE — I am not qualified enough

THE JALILA STORY
JALILA — If I work hard enough, I will be rewarded

THE NIKKI STORY
NIKKI — I'm okay in the background

continuum. First, you become aware of what is in the way. Then you slowly allow your light to shine brighter by taking a small step forward, rewriting the mindset that is shown in the yellow zone. Next is moving toward the green zone, which will allow you to tap into the power within. Green means growth. Green means GO – full speed ahead to unleash the best side of yourself.

Each sister will be revealed one at a time, but here is a look at where we are going. See page 266 for complete chart or download at YourLionInside.com.

KARI	THE KARI STORY I expect perfection ▶	▶	
RANEE	THE RANEE STORY I have to meet all demands ▶	▶	
GABRIELLA	THE GABRIELLA STORY I need permission/approval ▶	▶	
DARSHA	THE DARSHA STORY I should accept what is said ▶	▶	
AVALENE	THE AVALENE STORY I am not qualified enough ▶	▶	
JALILA	THE JALILA STORY If I work hard enough, I will be rewarded ▶	▶	
NIKKI	THE NIKKI STORY I'm okay in the background ▶	▶	

Stop allowing these mindsets to stand in the way.   *Slowly* allow your light to shine brighter...   *Go* forward and unleash your best self!

Everyone will respond to the Sisterhood differently based on their past. For some, simply becoming aware of the mindsets standing in their way will be incredibly freeing. For them, change often happens like a light switch. The ah-ha moment shifts everything very quickly. For others, it will be much harder to see the need for change because they are still in the fishbowl.

Be patient with yourself. The pace at which you cycle through these mindsets depends on the amount of *pain* in your way, conscious or unconscious. There is no right or wrong way; there is only *your way*. Every win for yourself in breaking free from these illusions, no matter how small, is a win for you and your sisters.

And now, you are ready to meet each of the sisters.

The Kari Story

Kari is a busy momprenuer - a business owner who is actively balancing the role of mom and the role of entrepreneur. A 17-year marketing veteran, Kari owns two businesses, has three children (two under the age of 4) and a passion for cooking, her clients and generally over-extending herself. Her most recent business, a dating coaching company, has been featured in *Forbes* and *Business Insider*, and on several network news programs. She is a wise soul with big ideas to change the world. Her genuine, no-nonsense spirit endears her to clients. Her ambition, thirst for big ideas and willingness to drive results is what keeps this woman on the go.

"I have little kids who hate to eat - and I LOVE to cook and feed others. I call myself a 'social feeder'," says Kari. "So when our neighborhood held a potluck, I was all in. The prospect of having a whole group to cook for was exhilarating. Adults! People who would appreciate what I had to offer!"

Digging through an extensive recipe collection, Kari carefully selected a few of her best and set to work. The big day arrived and, as it so often happens, it ended up being a little crazier than expected. Her parents randomly stopped by for a short visit. At the last minute, her husband decided to go fishing, which translated into no one available to help watch the crazy kiddos. And before she even got to work making all the food she had promised, she had to stop by a friend's baby's birthday party (with an appropriate gift, of course) *and* she still had to run around in search of a few gourmet, hard-to-find ingredients for her fabulous recipes. Oh, and raspberries still needed to be gathered from the garden (her girls had already eaten her first harvest earlier in the day).

Kari was stretched thin to say the least. More accurately, she was stressed, exhausted and overcommitted. Yet she had grand plans to create a magnificent frozen masterpiece. What she didn't count on: her ice cream machine not working.

Here was her Facebook post the next morning –

> *"Friends, I am tired and it's my own dang fault. When it comes to feeding others, I go way overboard and it's going to kill me one of these days. Last night our neighborhood had a potluck party. Instead of being a normal person, I had to make 2 gallons of homemade, homegrown raspberry ice cream and 5 gallons of HOMEMADE root beer. The root beer was easy BUT it took time to track down all the ingredients (root beer extract, dry ice, etc. – things not generally laying around in my pantry).*
>
> *On top of that, I also volunteered to make the meat for the party. Naturally, I went with ribs, so think about all the prep time there too. Remember how I run two businesses and have tiny, crazy children too?*
>
> *Bottom line, I LOVE hosting things and feeding people but I need an intervention. Seriously though, next time I am going to bring some chips.*
>
> *I'm gonna go nap now.*

Can you relate?

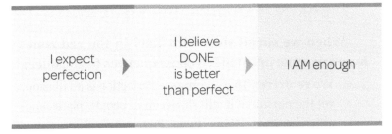

LIFE WITH KARI IN THE RED ZONE

When someone is in the red zone with Kari, these are the kinds of phrases you will hear:

- "It will take just a little extra time, really."
- "I am just trying to make sure everyone is taken care of."
- "I just can't help myself."
- "I'm sorry, I have not had time to . . ."
- "Sure, I can do that . . ."

This is the energy behind Kari in the red zone. Keep in mind it is often unspoken and unconscious. You have to pause long enough to look closely to realize what is going on.

- Purity of heart (albeit misguided at times)
- Never good enough
- Angst
- Striving

- Going the extra mile at a personal price
- Never-ending
- Exhausting
- Apologetic

LOOKING FARTHER DOWN THE ROAD

When we spend time with Kari in the red zone, here are some unintended consequences to consider:

- **We're driven to extremes** – Perfection is an illusion, yet the pursuit of it still shows up in people, places and circumstances. Think about Pinterest, endless photo editing apps and the quest for the ultimate image to share with the world.

- **We are never at peace in the present moment** – You strive to "do" more. The time building up to the "event" is filled with anxious energy to do everything just right. The time after the "event" is filled with longing for what you had hoped to do. Not to mention the enjoyment of the event itself is missed because you're not living in the present moment.

- **We waste time on things that won't matter in the long run** - The expectation for perfection adds unnecessary pressure to relationships and creates unrealistic expectations. All this leads to exhaustion once again, robbing those close to you of the best you have to offer.

- **Our children learn to focus on everyone and everything else** - Kari is very close to Ranee who strives to meet all demands. Our daughters internalize our desperate quest to make things "just right," creating a never-ending cycle.

- Is it possible that our expectations for perfection **set the stage for our sons to expect perfection in the future**? Are we unknowingly teaching our sons that women *will do it all*, a cycle which shows up in the future at work *and* at home?

LIFE IN THE GREEN ZONE

"I am enough"

When someone is in the green zone with Kari, here are the kinds of things you will hear:

- "All is well."

- "I've done enough already."

- "I am going to take care of myself this time."

- "It would be great to do 'x' but not this time."

- Silence – because no words are needed

This is the energy behind Kari living in the green zone. Keep in mind it is often unspoken; however, it radiates from the inside out. People notice but they are not sure why.

- Peaceful

- Calm

- Deep wisdom and understanding

- Breath of fresh air

- Accepting and in the *now*

- Shift from *doing* to *being*

- No longer has anything to prove

THE REST OF THE STORY: A FOLLOW-UP CONVERSATION WITH KARI

When did your ah-ha moment happen that motivated the Facebook post above? Did you laugh at yourself or cry?

> *My ah-ha moment came when I was sitting at the party. Everyone was having a great time. Except me. I was flustered that the ice cream was melting. People were not actually going to get to taste it and therefore praise me for it. I realized the next morning, as I was exhausted, sore and grumpy that my desire to "serve" others was really self-serving.*

Did you realize perfection was influencing you unconsciously?

> *Here's the thing - I would have never said I was a perfectionist. I rebel against the very concept! I have three kids— have you seen my house? I've learned my lessons around perfection paralysis in the past. I wouldn't consider myself or my motivations coming from perfectionism. Whenever I've met people who are perfectionists, it seemed like a condition they had. I didn't realize perfectionism can show up in circumstances!*

What was your biggest takeaway from this experience?

> *Next time I would rather be fed than dead.*

#theKaristory   #myKari

KARI

INSPIRATION ON THE JOURNEY TO FREEDOM

Affirmations

A powerful tool to reinforce your conscious desire to shift the way you think . . .

Perfection is an illusion.

I will pause long enough to ask myself, "Is this really necessary?"

I was made to be me – why be anyone else?

Today, I am enough.

The world needs me to be me.

Songs to Motivate You

"Strength, Courage & Wisdom" by India Arie

"A Rose is Still a Rose" by Aretha Franklin

"Q.U.E.E.N." by Janelle Monae

"Beautiful" by Christina Aguilera

"Born This Way" by Lady Gaga

Movies/Books to Energize You:

Gifts of Imperfection by Brené Brown

Moana

Wild: A Journey from Lost to Found by Cheryl Strayed

True Stories to Energize You

GreatBigStory.com – Search "Tangled Roots"

Youtube.com – Search "Why My Grey Hairs Make Me Happy"

Goalcast.com – Search "Mel Robbins – Felt Like a Complete Failure"

Youtube.com – Search "Oprah Winfrey Network: School of Awake"

The Ranee Story

Energetic and spunky, Ranee was a deep thinker, with loads of creativity and ambition. She had earned her MBA from a prestigious business school (where she was student council vice president of a college with 35,000 students, a leader in her sorority and a top academic) and was now working her way up through management positions with a healthcare giant.

She had boundless energy – an enviable trait, admirable as well, since she also had an equally energetic nine-month-old daughter. However, all that energy was misdirected. Ranee was always going 100,000 miles per hour, but not in any specific direction. Instead, she was doing everything in every area of her life: professional and personal. As one coworker said, "I want Ranee to know that she does not have to say *yes* to everything!"

Feedback from superiors suggested that Ranee "needed to harness her energy. She is very passionate but it can be overwhelming. She has a hard time learning to 'wait' for the right time."

Interestingly, additional feedback about Ranee was that "she didn't look the part" of an executive at the next level. Fair enough. But the commentary continued: "She is not able to spend much time on herself after having a baby." Sounds like the Narrative was working its toxic ways, doesn't it? After all,

75

can you imagine a sleepless new father receiving a similar assessment? This serves as a reminder: as you work on the mindsets of your internal world, the Narrative is still alive and well in the external world.

The higher-ups did see much potential in Ranee; they admired her ability to motivate others, her openness to learning and willingness to do whatever it took to climb the ladder. "She brings a lot of positive to the table . . . we see a long runway with her."

But somehow, despite her effort and output, it seemed Ranee was standing in her own way.

A few years ago, she was at company headquarters, working as one of the main architects of a massive $100 million deal. She had established quite a reputation for herself as being dangerously creative when it came to creating big deals that required new ways of thinking. "This deal was particularly important because it effected some of our largest clients," Ranee said. "Everyone was pressed for time and ideas as the pressure was on to reach the project goals on deadline."

The large team started early in the morning. Midday, a male manager, who was sitting next to Ranee, said, "It's almost lunch time, gang. I think we need to order."

Immediately, almost instinctively, Ranee jumped up and began taking lunch orders for the entire group. She remembers the day clearly because it offered a lesson she never forgot. "I was driving to Subway to fetch lunch for this room full of men and crying the whole way," she says. "I was in disbelief. After all these years and *all this hard work*, I was the person picking up lunch. It felt awful. I felt awful."

Her mind was racing. She thought about how little value she must provide to this group. The story she created in her head went downhill from there. It did not help that she had just returned from maternity leave. She began to wonder if maybe she wasn't needed while she was gone. Maybe she had not been as valuable as she thought. For days she made herself crazy thinking about things she could have done to avoid "being the person who gets lunch." It felt so powerless. She made her husband crazy too. Ranee was consumed by thinking of ways to muster up enough strength next time to say, "Yes, I am hungry too, let's have someone get us lunch." Why didn't she do that?

Fast forward one year, same company, another big deal. Ranee had since been promoted to the same level as the manager who had suggested lunch. And once again, he was sitting next to her at the meeting. She had just flawlessly delivered a strong idea that had heads nodding around the room. The manager turned to her, "That is really smart, Ranee." To which she quickly responded, "Thank you. I guess I can do more than get lunch." Confused, he asked her what she meant. She told him about being the one to get lunch a year ago. He laughed and said, "I was just hungry. I meant *someone* should get us lunch. I didn't mean you needed to be the one to do it."

| I have to meet all demands | ▶ | I CAN say no | ▶ | Here is what I am willing to do |

LIFE WITH RANEE IN THE RED ZONE

"I have to meet all demands."

When someone is in the red zone with Ranee, these are the kinds of phrases you will hear:

- "I'll do it!"

- "I can take care of that – no problem."

- "I will be glad to do that," – *sigh*.

- "I have a lot on my plate, but I guess *one more thing* won't matter."

- "I'm just trying to make it easier on everyone else."

This is the energy behind Ranee in the red zone. Keep in mind it is often unspoken. You have to pause and look closely to realize what is going on.

- Pressured
- Busyness is a distractor (from silence, life's problems, etc.)
- Victimhood
- Tethered to Kari and her worldview of perfection
- Taken advantage of
- Resentful at times
- Powerless

LOOKING FARTHER DOWN THE ROAD

When we spend time with Ranee in the red zone, here are some unintended consequences to consider:

- **We spin ourselves into exhaustion** – Many times the pressure on our shoulders is self-induced. The opportunity? Allow space for others to respond first. We don't have to race to save everyone all the time.

- **A vein of resentment builds over time** – The outcome of this is predictable. We will eventually explode or implode: an emotional breakdown, a physical illness or no interest in life. Slow down and ask why – *why am I doing this*? Life has seasons of busy-ness, but it is impossible to sustain forever. If we don't reign it in on our own terms, life has a way of doing it for us.

- **We rob others of their responsibilities**. When we build dependence on us, it removes the chance for others to learn. *Our doing everything actually hurts more than it helps in the long run.*

- **We teach our daughters to focus on the wrong things.** We unconsciously send our daughters the message they have to do it all, thus starting a new generation of a never-ending cycle. The good news is *we can stop the cycle.*

- **We teach our sons never to be truly independent** – Is it possible we have a hand in creating their expectation for women to do it all in the future – personally and professionally? As one mom said, "my son is getting married in a few days and still expects someone else to iron his military uniform - sigh."

LIFE IN THE GREEN ZONE

"Here is what I am willing to do."

When someone is in the green zone with Ranee, here are the kinds of things you will hear:

- "I will be glad to do 'x'; however, let's discuss the priorities . . ."
- "My schedule does not allow for 'x,' but it does allow for 'y'."
- "The best way I can be of help is to do _____."
- "Thank you for thinking of me, but my schedule does not permit this right now."
- "I look forward to being able to help in the future."

This is how it feels to hang out in the green zone with Kari (the energy behind it) –

- Empowered
- Strong
- Clarity

- Peaceful
- Victorious
- Respected

THE REST OF THE STORY: A FOLLOW-UP CONVERSATION WITH RANEE

What was it like to realize your biggest obstacle was an internal mindset?

> *It was a big eye-opener. I struggle with wanting to say yes to everyone for everything. Someone once told me there is a sense of power created when you say no to someone who is asking you to do a job you shouldn't be doing.*

Part of your journey has been making time to invest in YOU. That investment has translated into your professional success. Was it worth it?

> *Absolutely. I have rewired the way I think about many things. I recognize my mindset can mirror Jalila too. Once I became a mom – a working mom - I found it hard to prioritize self-care. It was impossible to do something as simple as get my hair blown out when I was making sure a diaper blow out wasn't on me when I left for work! I always had this belief that my body and appearance were simply a holder for my mind. I didn't realize that my outer polish affected my ability to influence others. While I am not one who will ever be fashion-forward, I did outsource the help I needed in this area. I found a service that rents beautiful professional clothing and one that rents jewelry. I didn't have to think about it. Now, I always look put together and it doesn't break the bank. I also cut my hair and made the look more professional. I was amazed at how much more influence I had once I looked the part*

of a trusted leader. By investing in myself on multiple levels, I finally earned the promotion I wanted. I increased my salary package by over 30%, which says a lot, considering I was already in the top tier. Small actions really do have big impact.

Considering all that you have learned on your journey, what advice would you pass on to other women?

First, consciously choose to **underreact**. *I find that many of our problems are actually the result of our reaction to situations, rather than the actual situations. Second, invest in yourself and your career. Hire people to do the busy work at home. Use that time to invest in your career, your family or your own free time. We have 168 hours each week. Even if you work 60 of those hours and sleep 56 hours, that still leaves 64 hours a week you can control. Keep a NOT-TO-DO list. . . and don't do the things that don't provide you value. Finally, pick your metrics for how you will measure success. I used to be so upset that I couldn't put my daughter to bed every night. The metric of being home every night was impossible to hit. My favorite part of bedtime is reading books to her. So I changed the metric. Now my goal is to read my daughter 14 books per week. If I miss a night, I make it up in the morning or over the weekend.*

What wisdom do you want to pass on to your daughter?

I want my daughter to know that she doesn't have to be a perfect mom or a perfect employee. My mom tells this story from when I was 8 years old: she got a call at work from the police. They said the house had been broken into. Mom went running home to find the house was not broken into at all. She had left the window open. And our house was just its normal mess. That sometimes happens with a working mom who is too busy to clean the house!

#theRaneestory #myRanee

RANEE

INSPIRATION ON THE JOURNEY TO FREEDOM

Affirmations

A powerful tool to reinforce your conscious desire to shift the way you think . . .

I don't "have" to do anything.

It is no one else's responsibility to take care of me.

Caring for myself IS caring for others.

My "yes" is a gift - I will offer it wisely.

I am enough without the "doing."

Songs to Motivate You

"Defying Gravity" from Wicked

"No" by Meghan Trainor

"Golden" by Jill Scott

"You Don't Own Me" by Lesley Gore

Movies/Books to Energize You:

The Devil Wears Prada

Mona Lisa Smile

Norma Rae

True Stories to Inspire You

Youtube.com – Search "CBS News Q & A Melinda Gates"

GreatBigStory.com – Search "The Art of Childbirth"

http://99u.adobe.com/videos/55965/
liz-jackson-designing-for-inclusivity

The Gabriella Story

Gabriella's career was at a turning point. At 48, she was still haunted by the sudden loss of a job years earlier in her career. Despite having been a successful supervisor, when the time came to let someone go, she was the chosen one, even though she was also the only one with the requisite engineering degree. Was it because she was a woman? Was it because she was African-American? "No," her employees told her. "It's because you don't play the game. You care too much about us and the higher-ups don't like it."

The loss devastated her. Six years of her life dedicated to the company only to have it end with the rug being yanked out from under her unexpectedly. *I did everything they asked me to do*, she believed. *Is learning to play the game the only way I can succeed professionally?* A dark cloud descended over her enthusiasm. That experience planted seeds of doubt, which then led to her second-guessing herself at every turn.

Fast-forward almost a decade. Her career had been like a roller coaster – lots of ups and downs. Occasionally mentors showed up, guiding Gabi when possible. "Build your network," the mentors would remind her. A tough boss, countless tears shed, and 50 pounds heavier, Gabi had serious doubts about whether or not professional success was really worth it. She continued to hold on, by a thread. She now had two young children and life's priorities were pulling her in different directions. "Walking the fence, I had convinced myself that I would never fit in."

In 2013, Gabi attended a workshop sponsored by the Women's Network where she was introduced to the concept of *jumping into the driver's seat* of her career. It made total sense, and it was something she could do. So Gabi started making changes, slowly at first. One of those changes was to invest energy in herself again. She wanted to appear polished – an attempt to erase the lingering doubt that still clouded her confidence. She was tired of placing everyone else ahead of her own self-care.

In 2016, Gabi showed up at another women's event where I was one of the speakers. It was in the Building Your Leadership Brand session where participants learned about mindsets and how to change them. Gabi did not realize it but she was finally ready to shift an internal mindset which had been holding her back all these years.

After my session, Gabi came up to me. She told me about the internal battle she was fighting when it came to office politics. How paralyzed she felt, and again, asking herself if it was all worth it. "Kim, I don't know if I can do it anymore," she said. "Do you have any advice about how I should handle the politics? I am so tired of not being me." What Gabi didn't verbalize was how the internal battle was draining her spirit. One conversation was all it took to see how tired, worn-out and demotivated she was. It was obvious she had so much talent to offer but she had unknowingly placed herself in a cage, thinking she could not step out. *Why is she waiting for permission*? I wondered. *Why is she acting like a kitten when she has the strength of a lion trapped inside?*

"Gabi, has it ever occurred to you that maybe you don't have to change who you are? That it is quite possible *you* are meant to change *the culture*? Don't allow the environment to define you. You have the power to redefine it," I said.

In that moment, Gabi began to see her career through a different lens. She realized that she did not have to *navigate* politics; she had the power to *change* the politics. "That ah-ha moment was transformational. It was like I was hit over the head," Gabi said. Her newfound confidence propelled her into situations where she was able to demonstrate her unique skillset. On one occasion, she was able to fix a problem because she saw it differently than the others, and she saved her company $77 million in the process.

"At the end of the day, I embraced the fact that I was uniquely suited to do what was needed during times of enormous change. I started to focus on gaps in the company and took initiative, despite the fact that I did not fit the "mold" of what company execs looked like," Gabi said.

When she was asked about her interest in future positions, she boldly rose to the occasion. "I want executive-level growth," she stated. "I know I probably can't check off the boxes required, but I don't feel like the rules apply to me. I am not being arrogant. I am simply confident that the business model is changing and needs to invest in people like me." Much to her surprise, the senior leader AGREED and things have not been the same since. Gabi has been asked to lead assignments all over the world, and she is on the fast track to the executive level she now realizes she deserves. It is an exciting time and her confident energy radiates from the inside out.

It has been less than one year since she gave herself "permission" to shift the way she viewed company politics. Turns out, she didn't need a year. She had the power all along.

A Message From Kim

YourLionInside.com Video 3

I need permission/ approval	>	I TRUST my own decisions	>	I can move forward *in* confidence

LIFE WITH GABI IN THE RED ZONE

"I need permission/approval."

When someone is in the red zone with Gabi, these are the kinds of phrases you will hear:

- "I'm just trying to do . . ."
- "I'm not sure if I can do it."
- "Maybe I am not in the right place."
- "I am so tired of waiting for . . ."
- "Won't they ever change?"

This is the energy behind Gabi in the red zone. Keep in mind it is often unspoken. You have to pause and look closely to realize what is going on.

- Powerless
- Caged in
- Doubtful
- Controlled by others
- Anger or apathy

- Uncertainty
- Not measuring up
- Apologetic
- Vulnerable

LOOKING FARTHER DOWN THE ROAD

When we spend time with Gabriella in the red zone, here are some unintended consequences to consider:

- **Powerlessness begins to slip in but we don't realize it** - We grow weary of yearning for things to be different. We tend to question ourselves wondering what we are doing wrong. The self-doubt is rooted in Kari's expectation of perfection.

- **Resentment grows as time slips by** – The resentment bubbles up in odd places, surprising everyone, including ourselves. Professional unhappiness often spills over into personal life and vice versa. We feel our energy draining. We wonder why we have lost our zest for life.

- **We teach our daughters to wait** – We teach them to hold back and look for someone else to give them permission to move forward. We unconsciously communicate that's just "the way things are done." Over time, powerlessness seeps in as our girls wonder why the world seems more challenging each day.

- **We teach our daughters not to trust their own decisions** - We unconsciously send the message that the opinions of others are more important than their own.

- When our sons see us waiting for permission/approval, it becomes the norm. **They eventually become 'blinded' to gender issues.** They move forward in life *unaware* of the need to consciously value both men <u>and</u> women.".

LIFE IN THE GREEN ZONE

"I can move forward in confidence."

When someone is in the green zone with Gabriella, here are the kinds of things you will hear:

- "I don't know what I was waiting for."
- "I know deep down what to do."
- "I don't have to search for the answer outside anymore."
- "My confidence is unshakable now."
- "I can't wait for the future to unfold."

This is how it feels to hang out in the green zone with Gabriella's (the energy behind it)—

- Freedom
- Bold
- Love of self
- Worthy
- Empowered

- Energized
- Excited
- Possibilities
- Resolute
- Purposeful

THE REST OF THE STORY: A FOLLOW-UP CONVERSATION WITH GABI

What was it like to realize the biggest thing standing in your way was an internal mindset? Did you even realize you were waiting for permission or approval?

> *I had no idea I was waiting for permission, but it all makes sense now. Self-doubt had unconsciously become a part of my narrative when I was laid off in the previous role. I had to figure out how to do this job and be me. The self-speak is so crucial to your success. Once I changed my internal dialogues, things really did start changing for me.*

What did it feel like when you started to step into that personal power after your ah-ha moment? What might it look like to someone who is still stuck?

> *If you're comfortable, then you're stuck. Get challenged to grow in your business, expand your expertise or expand your impact. You must realize what you can do better than anyone else in your business. If you don't have that, get it - get it for yourself. It's not until you realize your value that you walk in it. Be the expert that you seek.*

The happiness and shock in your voice when you shared the exciting growth on your journey was amazing. You said you wanted "other women to realize their true potential and not doubt themselves." What words of encouragement do you have for your sisters on a similar journey?

> *The light comes on when you know your worth to the business and to yourself. The light comes on*

when you make a decision to turn it on. Once the light comes on, each of us can illumine the darkness. Even when you seem to be losing, it may set you up for your biggest win. Once I understood me and what made me, I started walking in my power. I have not looked back since. I'm now owning my value, my confidence, my strength, my purpose and doing the right thing for the business. I trust my own decisions more than ever.

In light of what you have learned on your journey over the past few years, what are some of the biggest lessons you hope to teach your sons about a woman owning her power?

You must give yourself grace and the ability to be you, being powerful. My parents are from a generation where it was ok to be the status quo and fit in. I now know that being me is more important than fitting in. I teach my boys to own their power. I tell them they do not have to be like mommy or daddy. Own your strengths and know that your strengths will change over time.

I'm all about legacy right now for my kids and grandkids. I want to have a network that will enable my kids to be powerful and own their strengths when they choose their life path. I know that I won't be able to provide everything for them, but I want to know who I can call to help them as they progress in life. I'm all about connection, legacy, and abundance. I want to listen to what's not being said when I meet a person and how I can fulfill that unspoken question, desire, or passion they don't know how to vocalize! I want that connection to translate into a life lesson for my lineage that will ultimately result in abundance for them - spiritually, mentally, emotionally, physically and financially. Ultimately, I want them to be able to move forward in confidence, no matter what happens in life.

#theGabistory   #myGabi

GABRIELLA

INSPIRATION ON THE JOURNEY TO FREEDOM

Affirmations

A powerful tool to reinforce your conscious desire to shift the way you think . . .

I choose to trust my own decisions.

Owning my power requires no apology.

I have gifts to bring to the world.

I choose to get out of my own way.

I got this.

Songs to Motivate You

"Freedom" by Beyonce

"Confident" by Demi Levato

"Stronger (What Doesn't Kill You)" By Kelly Clarkson

"The Greatest Love of All" by Whitney Houston

"Grateful" by Rita Ora

Movies/Books to Energize You:

Erin Brockovich

Black

GI Jane

True Stories to Energize You

GreatBig Story.com – Search "Nigeria's First Female Mechanic"

Ted.com – Search "A Saudi Woman Who Dared to Drive"

GreatBigStory.com – Search "Graffiti Grandma Destroys Hate"

The Darsha Story

I SHOULD ACCEPT WHAT IS SAID

Darsha works for a global company with high expectations for their leaders. Emotional intelligence, agility and self-discipline are a given. Leaders must have a thirst for excellence, a relentless pursuit of innovation and an endless reservoir of energy. Darsha had all of that and more.

"My boss said the leadership team did not feel I was ready for a team manager role. I am so frustrated! I moved my family all the way across the country to help launch this site. What else do I have to do to show I am committed to my career?" said Darsha.

Darsha, 34 years old and a mother of three, was her family's primary breadwinner. And on paper, things looked good: she was working with one of the most recognizable brands in the world. Her company was experiencing lightning growth across multiple industries, creating a blueprint for how to thrive in a digital world. Her bachelor of arts in history was an unlikely admission ticket into the wild west of the digital jungle. However, Darsha's expertise in research, sales and operations support put her on the fast track to success. For five years, she poured her heart and soul into her career waiting for the right opportunity. Finally, it arrived.

Darsha was invited to take on the intense challenge of launching a new site halfway across the country. After much thought and convincing - *it will lead to advancement soon*, she promised her husband - she made the difficult decision to relocate her entire family. With high hopes for a bright future, they left all family ties behind and headed west.

Months passed and no word of advancement. Not even a whisper. No matter how hard she worked, Darsha was beginning to wonder if she would ever move up that ladder. It seemed like no matter what she did, it was never enough for her boss and the leadership team. *Did I move my family across country for something that was never going to happen? Did I take a lateral career change for nothing?* Darsha wondered.

She had believed there would be tremendous career growth for those who got in early at this new site in her new home state. However, all of her attempts to discuss applying for higher-level positions were met with "you're not ready" or "we don't think you're operating on that level yet."

These frustrations were still fresh on her mind when she attended a company sponsored International Women's Conference in April of 2017. Attending a breakout session focused on the mindsets that hold women back in leadership, Darsha heard a statement that changed her life. "One of the mindsets was *I should accept what is said,*" she marveled. "That statement hit me like a two-by-four over the head. Yes, I did walk into that conference feeling powerless – like a victim. But I left with renewed determination to rewrite my narrative."

Darsha started this rewrite by approaching her advancement much more strategically. She gathered the statistics that would speak to the impact she had had on the new site. She requested new meetings with her boss and members of the leadership team. In essence, she took ownership of crafting her own narrative: one focused on all the skills she brought to the table and all that she had accomplished beyond the short year she'd been at the site.

"Darsha, I had no idea you had done all this. Why didn't you tell us before now?" asked her boss. While the position she originally wanted had been given to another, a project opportunity came up unexpectedly. This quasi-advancement provided an opportunity to showcase her skills. She was able to prove that she was ready for the promotion she had been seeking all along.

Four short months after the women's conference, Darsha's boss called her into his office. He shared the good news: she received the promotion. "You might want to sit down before you open that offer envelope," he said. "I could not believe my eyes," Darsha said. "It was a 66% increase over what I was making before. I can't tell you how life-changing this was for my family. I guess moving across the country paid off. And to think, I could have missed it if I had simply accepted what was said."

Her sisters nod in agreement. "Amazing what can happen when you tap into the power within."

| I should accept what is said | ▶ | I CAN pause, reflect and choose | ▶ | I choose to rewrite the narrative |

LIFE WITH DARSHA IN THE RED ZONE

"I should accept what is said."

When someone is hanging out with this side of Darsha, these are the kinds of phrases you will hear:

- "Well, okay, I guess so."
- "I guess I should just accept what my boss said."
- "I am beginning to wonder if things will ever change."
- "Am I the only one who feels this way? Ugh!"
- "Why do *they* do or say that, ugh?!?"

This is how it feels to hang out in the red zone with Darsha (the energy behind it) –

- Powerless
- Lack of belief in self
- Enslaved
- Trapped
- Tired
- Resentful
- Doubtful of one's ability
- Hopeless
- Confined
- Misunderstood
- Longing for freedom
- Apathetic
- Resigned

LOOKING FARTHER DOWN THE ROAD

When we spend time with Darsha in the red zone, here are some unintended consequences to consider:

- **Our success is kept in a holding pattern** - We find ourselves held hostage by the Narrative. We know we have more potential but are unsure how to unleash it. We become adept at talking ourselves out of what we really want and settling for much less – personally and professionally.

- **We no longer trust ourselves** – Our gut or intuition sends signals that something isn't right but we are often paralyzed. Self-doubt takes over. We find ourselves confined by the "everyone else believes it" bias.

- **Our daughters watch us accept when others place us in a box** – They wonder, *are we supposed to do the same?* This leads to teaching our daughters to follow the rules, no matter what. To be a good girl. Our daughters learn to be hesitant to push back. This rule-following mentality impacts the rest of their life, especially in the professional world, where taking risks is rewarded.

- **We are unconsciously trapped by the Narrative** - We model for our sons the type of responses they should expect from women, personally and professionally. We actually perpetuate the cycle of "this is way things are done," ultimately becoming a partner in keeping the Narrative alive.

LIFE IN THE GREEN ZONE

"I choose to rewrite the narrative."

When someone is in the green zone with Darsha, here are the kinds of things you will hear:

- "I have the power to change this."

- "Here is what I am going to do. I am not waiting on 'x' any longer."

- "Well – let's see about that."

- "I am not waiting for someone else to do 'x' anymore."

- "It feels like the wool is gone from my eyes – wow."

This is how it feels to hang out in the green zone with Darsha (the energy behind it) -

- Empowered
- Hopeful
- Brave
- Proud
- Growth
- High frequency
- Freedom of expression
- Respected
- Joyful
- Growth and abundance
- Fueled and charged
- Enlightened
- Expansive
- Complete
- Renewed energy

The #MeToo movement is rooted in the red zone of Darsha. As we watch the power of the movement unfold, keep in mind it addresses only one of the seven mindsets the Sisterhood has revealed. Imagine what our world will look like once we are able to shift all seven, individually and collectively.

Can you describe the ah-ha moment at the conference when you realized Darsha resonated with you?

My ah-ha moment came when we broke into small groups at the conference. We were asked to have different conversations based on the red, yellow, and green mindset of the sisters so we could see the self-fulfilling prophecy in action. Our table happened to have Darsha as the sister we were describing. Right before the exercise started, I had been talking with the table about my frustration with my manager and my career. I had ended my sentence with "Well I guess I just need to accept what they're telling me." When we were assigned Darsha everyone at the table gasped and said, "Oh my gosh - it's you!" They had me lead the discussion on how I felt currently, and then had me walk through the steps to rewrite my own narrative. It was powerful!

What was that session like to realize perhaps the thing standing in your way was an internal mindset?

I felt completely blown away as I started thinking about this differently. Once I questioned why I was simply accepting what I was told, I finally saw the path clearly. I felt energized and it lit a fire inside of me to go after what I wanted. As women, we're taught to be assertive, not aggressive. I felt like I had been assertive, but still wasn't getting anywhere. So it really made me feel empowered that I could be more intentional – even aggressive - with what I wanted. I had the power to

> explain what I had accomplished in my career and revisit the promotion opportunity with my boss. I had assumed he knew all of my skills. It ended up that he had no idea of all the things I had done before I started working with him. That was a BIG lesson for me! The experience taught me that it's okay to look at things differently and not to be afraid to push back.

What did it feel like when you started to step into that personal power? What might it look like to someone who might still be stuck?

> I felt powerful and hopeful. When I was stuck, I was spending a lot of time blaming others: "How can they not see all that I've done?!" "I'm already doing X, Y, and Z, what more do they need me to do to show I'm ready?!"

> If you are trying to advance your career and find yourself uttering phrases that sound powerless, like I did, it's time to take a hard look at yourself. Ask yourself, "What have I shown my manager about this, this, and this project? Does my manager know I implemented this process change and it resulted in our metrics exceeding targets by X amount?"

> It is important to remember that no one is a mind reader. Simply because they are your manager/boss doesn't mean they know everything you've done. It's important to be an advocate for yourself and be your own cheerleader, like Jalila's green zone.

You have been inspired to share your excitement with other women so they can change their lives too. Once the light dawns that there is a new reality, we can't contain our excitement to encourage our sisters. What do you want to share with them?

So often women internalize the message they are to be seen and not heard. Unfortunately, this really filters into our careers. For me, it's about encouraging women to be more vocal about what they want. That being seen as intentional in your goals isn't a bad thing. I've become so passionate about developing women's careers that I've started a women's chapter at my site. Our main focus is career development. I'm already starting to see an impact on other women. I've helped with resume reviews, interview prep, and career development planning. It's great to see so many women get excited about their careers.

#theDarshastory   #myDarsha

DARSHA

INSPIRATION ON THE JOURNEY TO FREEDOM

Affirmations

A powerful tool to reinforce your conscious desire to shift the way you think . . .

I am writing my life story - day by day, decision by decision.

Change my words, change my world.

I no longer fear the unknown; I courageously embrace it.

Look out world, here I come!

My courage will open doors – for me and others.

Songs to Motivate You

"Fighter" by Christina Aguilera

"Feeling Good" by Nina Simone

"Shake It Off" by Taylor Swift

"Roar" by Katy Perry

"Own It" by will.i.am

Movies/Books to Energize You

Hidden Figures

"These women had every reason to be competitive but instead they supported each other. My favorite part is when Octavia Spencer finds out about this new technology called a computer. Everyone feared for their jobs. Instead of accepting that fate, she got smart. She decided to learn more. She realized the computer would need programmers and her group would be ready when the time came. That spoke to me because so many people live in the past and want to hold on to how we've always done things. Instead of folding under pressure, she took ownership and said I am going to create an opportunity. I love that!" Angela R. 42 years young, Media Professional, Seattle, WA

The Help

Hope for the Flowers by Trina Paulus

True Stories to Inspire You

GreatBigStory.com – Search "Spain's All-female Cricket Team"

GreatBigStory.com – Search "Bodybuilding at 80 Years Old"

YouTube.com - Search "I Survived the Holocaust Twin Experience"

The Avalene Story

I'M NOT QUALIFIED ENOUGH

The solidly confident, graciously proud Avalene of today is quite different from the quiet, accommodating Avalene of the past. To fully appreciate how close she came to taking the path of least resistance, let us wind back the clock. . .

Growing up in a small town steeped in middle-class values, Avalene quickly learned that hard work and perseverance was the recipe for success. She worked her way through school and graduated with a bachelor's degree in business. Her first job led her down the path of IT, an ideal fit for her natural troubleshooting mind and problem-solving skills. She liked to think of herself as a modern-day Indiana Jones, searching for hidden treasures in a jungle of code. Steady, measured success was the linear formula she was taught. Move from Point A to Point B and then to Point C. *Don't get too far ahead of yourself* and *First, pay your dues* were the philosophies she internalized. Stability was the Holy Grail. Sure, at times, she sensed an internal battle within herself because she also wanted room to grow. Stability *and* growth – were they mutually exclusive or could you have both? Avalene wasn't sure of the answer, and she wasn't sure she was willing to risk finding out.

Her first job was good; however, due to an unstable economy, the company closed. *This time, I'll pick a better field,* she told herself: the solid stable of academia. So she moved several hours away to pursue an IT position with a legendary university. Yes, she was completely overqualified for the job, but Avalene was determined to do whatever it took to land in a place she could professionally call home. Even if that meant underselling herself. *Just for now*, she rationalized.

With a foot in the door, she settled in quickly and that was that . . . or so she thought. A year passed. Avalene's internal desire to grow demanded more and more attention, but controlled by the status quo mentality - you do things the proper, expected way – she continued to dismiss those growth impulses, although it was taking more and more conscious effort to do so.

Each week, she would look over her company's internal job postings, dismissing most opportunities as out of her league and passing over others because she did not have the "preferred" requirements. One week, however, one posting stopped her in her tracks. She read it over several times, each time talking herself out of the opportunity. The position required a lot of interaction with VPs and senior leaders. The sheer thought of interacting with executives at that level intimidated her. *I am still new in my field,* she told herself. *It is too much of a stretch for me.* More negative self-talk beat her down - *I should be grateful for the job I have already, I'm not sure I can do this* - and she talked herself right out of applying for the position.

Two months later, Avalene came face to face with what was holding her back from the growth she so desired. She was reading an article about how men and women approached the job application process differently. One sentence felt strangely familiar: "Women apply for jobs only when they have 100% of the qualifications, yet men apply when they have only 60% of the qualifications." *Why is that,* she wondered. *Don't they think they're qualified enough?* And then it hit her. That mindset – *I am not qualified enough* - was her internal battle.

One she realized exactly what was holding her back - a mindset - she knew it was time to change the way she thought. She finished reading the article and returned to work the following day with a renewed commitment to find the confidence to go after this stretch assignment. For three long months, she went through the interview process. Avalene studied and prepped harder than she ever had for another position. "I knew I had to get their attention so I did a lot of homework."

It was a Thursday afternoon. Avalene's phone rang and she saw it was the interviewer. *This is it,* she thought. Taking a deep breath, she picked up the phone. "We appreciated all of your effort - it was noted by everyone on the committee. But we have decided to go with someone who has more experience," he stated. After expressing her appreciation for the opportunity, Avalene asked sincerely, "What can I do differently next time?"

What was supposed to be a short five-minute talk turned into a fifteen-minute conversation. Avalene hung up, disappointed, but proud of herself for trying.

Friday morning, the phone rang, and she noticed it was the interviewer again. "I have thought about this all night and have revisited our decision about the position," he began. "Even though you don't have all the experience, I really do feel you are the right one for the position. Will you still consider our offer to hire you?" Surprised and elated, Avalene answered with an enthusiastic "yes!" and took a giant step into her new future.

| I am not qualified enough | ▶ | I AM the right one for the opportunity | ▶ | There is enough for me AND you |

LIFE WITH AVALENE IN THE RED ZONE

"I am not qualified enough."

When someone is hanging out with this side of Avalene, these are the kinds of phrases you will hear:

- "I should be grateful for the job I have already."
- "I'm not sure I can do this."
- "I am loyal to 'x' right now – there will be another opportunity later."
- "Should I or shouldn't I?" – signs of an internal battle.
- "I am not sure if I am ready for that yet."

This is how it feels to hang out in the red zone with Avalene (the energy behind it) –

- Lacking confidence or minimal confidence
- Whispering
- Wandering
- When is my turn?
- Distrusting of the future
- Jealousy
- Lacking
- Fearful
- Doubtful
- Pained
- Striving
- Petty
- Strife
- Unsure
- Uncomfortable

LOOKING FARTHER DOWN THE ROAD

When we spend time with Avalene in the red zone, here are some unintended consequences to consider:

- **Opportunities slip through our fingers** – All our actions are interdependent. When we advance, our sisters advance. This is a privilege of sisterhood, not a burden. Because we often love our sisters enough - often more than ourselves - this can give us courage.

- **We become paralyzed by our internal battles** - We unconsciously shift into a waiting mentality and grow restless. We start to feel unsettled, even unappreciated. We begin to wonder if we are in the right place. We wonder if we will ever have the confidence to move on. We are unaware that we have placed ourselves in a box, and we forget that we have the power to climb out.

- **Unknowingly, we send our daughters a message of low confidence** - We plant seeds of doubt: *If mom can't do it, how can I?* We teach our daughters to wait for opportunities instead of creating them. We perpetuate the myth that the formula for success *lies in someone else's hands* – not our own. The seeds of doubt plow fertile ground for the red zone of Nikki to take root (I'm okay in the background).

- **Sons can become trapped by believing they have to *save* mom** – When a mother believes she's not qualified and shifts into a mindset of powerlessness, her son steps in as the protector. Seeds of doubt are planted in these sons' minds about the ability of women in general. And as a result, some of these young boys grow into men who exert control over women, personally or professionally, due to this unconscious belief.

LIFE IN THE GREEN ZONE

"There is enough for me AND you."

When someone is in the green zone with Avalene, here are the kinds of things you will hear:

- "I can do this!"
- "I can learn anything I set my mind to."
- "I feel like a success story – wow!"
- "I look for opportunities to encourage other women now."
- "I can't help but share with women that there is another way!"

This is how it feels to hang out in the green zone with Avalene (the energy behind it) –

- Brave
- Proud
- Adventurous
- Daring
- Dreaming
- Self-assured
- Validated

- Hopeful
- Creative
- Solid
- Bold
- Gracious
- Energized
- Determined

THERE IS ENOUGH FOR ME AND YOU

Celebrating the success of another does not diminish our own. Celebrating the beauty of another does not diminish our own. The power lies in focusing on abundance. With each individual success, it is a building block for the foundation for the sisterhood collectively. Embrace the idea that your success is my success and my success is your success.

How were you feeling about life before you decided to go after
your dream job?

> *There was an internal battle going on inside my
> head. After all, I had been with the university just
> under a year. Who was I to think I could move on?
> Didn't I need to be loyal to the person who hired
> me in the first place? I could not see past the many
> roadblocks I placed in the way. Oddly enough, most
> of the roadblocks I imagined didn't even exist. We
> often make things harder than they have to be. I
> was very fragile going into the conversation with
> my boss at the time. Surprisingly, she was very en-
> couraging. What a relief! She inspired me to do the
> same for others from this point forward.*

What was it like to realize perhaps the biggest thing standing
in your way was an internal mindset?

> *It was so freeing to let go of the self-doubt.
> Persistence and determination have always been a
> part of my career plan but my internal doubts were
> burdensome. Learning how my mindset was hold-
> ing me back opened my eyes; it was educational
> and motivational. The time span between becoming
> "aware" of my mindset and my shift to do something
> about it was very short. It was like the light turned
> on in my head. I'm really not sure I would have ap-
> plied for my dream job had I not gained this aware-
> ness. I might still be in the red zone today waiting
> for "my turn."*

Your story has been so inspiring as you have stayed in touch along the journey. The sisterhood is all about spreading the energy to empower other women to break free from their self-imposed limitations. Any words of wisdom to encourage other women?

*If you want something, don't talk yourself out of it. Surprisingly, other women began to reach out to me while I was going through the three-month interview process. They kept asking, "What did you do to move yourself forward?" I shared that **I had to get out of my own way**! I also gave way too much power to the "preferred master's degree" qualification. Don't allow yourself to get stuck on the preferred qualifications. Instead, focus on the value you bring to the table. You get an entirely different outcome when you shift your focus. I love my job now and it has exceeded my expectations. This position bumped me to a 64% increase once I included my benefits. I want other women to experience the same success!*

#theAvalenestory   #myAvalene

AVALENE

INSPIRATION ON THE JOURNEY TO FREEDOM

Affirmations

A powerful tool to reinforce your conscious desire to shift the way you think . . .

I have an innate ability to learn and grow.

Fear has no place in my world.

I am already a success – the rest of the world will catch up soon.

I choose to be brave.

My footsteps will lead others down a brave path someday.

Songs to Motivate You

"Salute" by Little Mix

"I'm Coming Out" by Diana Ross

"I'm Every Woman" by Whitney Houston

"You Will (The Own Song)" by Jennifer Hudson and Jennifer Nettles

Movies/Books to Energize You:

Mean Girls

The Secret Life of Bees by Sue Monk Kidd

A League of Their Own

True Stories to Inspire You

GreatBigStory.com – Search "All Female Sushi House"

Starbucks.com – Search "Upstanders: A Racist's Rehabilitation"

GreatBigStory.com – Search "Instigators the Midwife of La Cienega Boulevard"

The Jalila Story

IF I WORK HARD ENOUGH, I WILL BE REWARDED

The unexpected call came late one Friday afternoon.

"I am so frustrated right now, Kim, I don't know what to do. Over the years, I've hired you to help many other leaders at this company. Now, I'm calling about me," Jalila, a leader I had worked with for well over a decade, said. "I just found I didn't receive the pay increase I'd been promised. *For the third year in a row!* Can you please, please help me see what I am missing?"

Always on the go, Jalila had major responsibilities in a luxury brand currently experiencing double-digit growth. She had already invested fourteen years in the company, growing their professional development division. Well-respected and known for making things happen, Jalila was able to accomplish more than most. Her drive, expertise and quest for excellence made her essential to the North American site.

However, Jalila was so focused on *doing* the job that she missed the signs as the company slowly boxed her into exactly where they needed her to be. It took the third time of not being recognized for her to make that Friday afternoon call to me. Literally, and figuratively, she had reached the end of her rope.

What else did she have to do to be recognized? Her frustration was driven by many unanswered, and unspoken, questions.

The good news was this crisis stopped Jalila in her tracks long enough to invest much needed time into herself. She had fallen into the trap of thinking *if I work hard enough, I will be rewarded.* The strategy had worked for many years early in her career. However, her professional life "grew up" and reached a predictable point where hard work alone was no longer enough.

"When is the last time you invested in your success – your leadership brand, Jalila?" I asked.

"Invest in myself?" she laughed out loud. "Who has time for that? I have work to do!"

For over ten minutes, she adamantly explained *all* the responsibilities she had, *all* the tasks she had completed and the growing pressure of *all* the expectations now squarely placed upon her shoulders. "Don't you realize this is the *third* boss I have had in five years? While those leaders are coming and going, I am the one left running this place. There has been no time to invest in me."

The rest of our conversation was uncomfortable. Jalila listened as I explained that the very mindsets which had made her successful up to this point were not enough to take her to the next level. "It's time to focus on increasing your visibility instead of simply working hard," I said. Hesitantly she considered the possibility that it *was* time to think differently. Not completely convinced but willing to try, she agreed to spend the next three months investing in herself.

"This is not going to be easy. I don't like talking about myself. I am not sure this is really the problem. If the bosses would just do their job," she muttered.

"Time will tell," I calmly replied.

Over the next three months, Jalila begrudgingly worked to raise her visibility. With each small step, she started to see things change. Leaders would spend more time with her once she arranged a meeting asking for their insight. Each action was a stepping stone to a new path. Even when she saw progress, she was quick to revert back to "do these things really matter? I just want to do my job." She was not one to waste money, but if the company was investing in having me as her coach, she was going to use the advice. The day arrived when she called about a retreat she was facilitating for upper management. She reached out requesting ideas about how to do it well.

"Now that you have the mechanics planned out, what are you going to do to invest in YOUR leadership brand while you are there?" I asked. "How can you use this opportunity as a way to authentically raise your visibility?"

Jalila sighed loudly. "I had not thought of that. Do I really need to? After all, they are there for the retreat, not to listen to me," she hastily explained.

"It is exactly that mindset that led to your not receiving a well-deserved increase for the third year in a row," I reminded her. Silence.

A few moments later, she begrudgingly signed on to my suggestion. "Fine. So how do I do it in a low-key way?"

Strategy in place, her low-key effort worked. Every time she experienced a small success, her confidence grew. Each time her confidence grew, leaders responded positively. Jalila started to believe small actions have big impact.

During this process, we stumbled upon a key leverage, which was glaringly obvious once Jalila thought about it. It was so obvious she had missed it for the last three years. It was the promotion process: each year, the bosses would gather in a room to discuss the list of employees who were in line for an increase. Only a certain number of increases were allowed each year – and those limited increases went to the people whose leaders were able to speak the loudest, influence the most or offer the most compelling case for why their employee was so deserving.

"Jalila, what have you done to prepare your new boss to be able to fight on your behalf when this process starts again?" I asked.

"Nothing. I have done nothing because I assume that, as the boss, they know what to do," Jalila said.

"How can your new boss know what to say on your behalf when you can't even describe to me the value you bring? You are so valuable to the division that many would have difficulty clearly articulating what you do, much less do it in a compelling way." It was becoming clear to us both that perhaps one of the reasons her bosses kept changing - being promoted - was *because* of her hard work. One look at Jalila and I saw the light-bulb come on. And from that moment on, everything shifted.

Less than ninety days later, I received another, very different phone call. "Amazing news – I received the pay grade increase this time!" *You go Jalila,* I thought. *Don't stop now.*

Luckily, she didn't. Eighteen months later, Jalila finally busted out of the box that she unknowingly allowed the company to place her in. She was promoted to a new division with fresh responsibilities. This is what happens when a talented woman finally begins to own and articulate her value. Good thing too. At 53, she still has a long runway ahead.

If I work hard enough, I will be rewarded	▶	I can advocate and CARE for myself	▶	I own and articulate my value

LIFE WITH JALILA IN THE RED ZONE

"If I work hard enough, I will be rewarded."

When someone is hanging out with this side of Jalila, these are the kinds of phrases you will hear:

- "I'm just trying to do my job."
- "Can't talk right now. I am on deadline." (every time you talk to her)
- "I don't have time to do things for myself. Do you know how much I have on my plate?"
- "I will take care of it. I always do. . ."
- "No one around here seems to realize how hard I work."

This is how it feels to hang out in the red zone with Jalila (the energy behind it) –

- Busyness (which can blind you to the root cause)
- Heavy
- Burdened
- Doubtful
- Questioning
- Distrustful
- Waiting
- Resentful
- Tired
- Victimhood
- Bitter

LOOKING FARTHER DOWN THE ROAD

When we spend time with Jalila in the red zone, here are some unintended consequences to consider -

- **We train everyone around us to expect it** – Unknowingly, our behavior teaches others to allow a disproportionate amount of work to be placed on our laps. They watch as we work ourselves to exhaustion. It is predictable that eventually, we will reach a point where we are tired of it! Only we don't realize that in many cases, we did it to ourselves.

- **We lose sight of the bigger picture** – With our heads down, doing the work becomes the short-term focus as we move from one event to the next. Teaching our children – or others – dependence on us today does not create fertile ground for independence in the future.

- **We pass on a lack of self-care** – Somehow, we have missed the pearl of wisdom that caring for ourselves IS caring for others. Caring for ourselves is an inside job *first*. As within, so without. The root of the issue is self-respect. We will never receive what we are not willing to give to ourselves.

- **We turn away help unnecessarily** – When others offer help, we often turn it away under the misguided notion that we have to work harder. We can learn to say yes. After all, care has a hidden message for us –

> **C**herish and
>
> **A**ccept
>
> **R**espect and support
>
> **E**very time it is offered!

LIFE IN THE GREEN ZONE

"I own and articulate my value."

When someone is in the green zone with Jalila, here are the kinds of things you will hear:

- "Owning my value gets easier and easier."
- "I don't wait for anyone else anymore."
- "I definitely feel more confident."
- "I take more risks – you never know what might happen."
- "I feel so much happier and free now."

This is how it feels to hang out in the green zone with Jalila (the energy behind it) -

- Understood
- Complete
- Tall
- Bold
- Self-full
- Clarity of thought and purpose
- Confident
- Still
- Alive and vibrant
- Tower of strength
- Unshakable
- Strong foundation

TO ALL OF THE JALILAS . . .

When we are dancing with Jalila, busy-ness becomes a major blind spot. It is not easy to connect the dots because investing in <u>ourselves</u> is not considered an important item on our "to do" list. This is a key characteristic found every single time Jalila's red zone shows up. The follow-up story below captures the essence of this quality.

THE REST OF THE STORY:

PART I: THE CONVERSATION *BEFORE* THE FOLLOW-UP CONVERSATION WITH JALILA

As you read Jalila's comments below, pay attention to what is *not* being said. Note how Jalila's ability to own and articulate her value has become a more natural state. So much so, she is hesitant to consciously admit that the reason things changed was because she changed her own mindset. Had there not been an outsider – me - observing the process, this lesson might have been missed entirely.

After several failed attempts to schedule a lunch with Jalila to reconnect, email was my only option. I emailed her the following in August of 2017: "I have been trying to connect with you over the past few months to let you know how your story has inspired other women. When time permits, I would love to explain. For now, I have to finish the book. I would like to include your story as part of a compilation – no names or companies listed. I know your gut may say no, but please hear me out."

Her email response came the next day. "Thanks for thinking of me. I am fine with you using me in a 'compilation format' – actually, *honored* is the best word." She then proceeded to explain her current busyness and how she had no time right now to talk further. She asked if we could connect in three months. *Some things never change,* I thought to myself with a smile. Hesitant to mention that the book would be published by then, I asked if we could correspond further through email. I had done this with other signature stories and the email format worked well: each woman was very forthcoming, open and honest, writing me lengthy, insightful responses.

PART II: A FOLLOW-UP
CONVERSATION WITH JALILA

I emailed the same three questions to Jalila. Here are my questions and her responses:

1. When you called that Friday afternoon in 2015 after receiving news of not receiving the pay increase for the third year in a row, how were you feeling?

> Jalila: Taken advantage of, mostly, and underappreciated.

2. How did it feel to go through the process of learning how to advocate for yourself?

> Jalila: It was a struggle. It felt unnatural and not me.

3. What does it feel like now that you are seeing the results of a shift in your perspective?

> Jalila: I don't think I really changed or I can't recognize it if I did. I just decided to do what was best for me and let go of other expectations. It is so freeing.

Knowing Jalila like I did, I requested a telephone conversation to uncover more of the story. I knew busyness sometimes kept her from connecting the dots. I also knew Jalila did not like talking about herself and that, deep down, she was probably wondering if her story could even make a difference.

After many weeks of pursuit, I finally caught up with her. She was at the airport, waiting for a flight which had been delayed. I had already dug out my files from years ago to remind her of how our conversations used to be, so I was ready . . . "Jalila, I promise to make this quick. I know there is more to the story than what you emailed. It is going to be important for other women to hear your entire story in order to learn from it."

"Alright, if you say so, Kim," she said, and proceeded to *really* answer my three questions.

PART III: A REAL CONVERSATION WITH JALILA

"How did it feel to go through the process of learning to advocate for yourself? You went into that process kicking and screaming."

> *Ha ha, yes that sounds quite familiar. When we started the coaching process, I felt taken advantage of and underappreciated. I had invested a lot of my life in making the company successful. I was tired and not sure if it was even possible for me to work any harder. I did not want to leave but I did wonder if that was going to be the only way I could advance.*
>
> *As for what changed, I simply started feeling more confident about myself through the process. I started working at a higher level and exposing myself to senior managers. I started taking more risks, which led to more successes. Putting myself out there made a big difference. By the time this current position opened up, I went for it! You know, now that I think about it, maybe it did result from my thinking differently . . . (sound like the self-fulfilling prophecy in action?).*

What does it feel like today, now that you shifted your perspective and became more comfortable acknowledging your value?

I finally learned to see through the bias. Others were resistant to my taking on this new position. I realized they were looking out for themselves, that they had their own interest at heart, not mine. I reached a point where I was confident enough to say to myself I don't care. I needed to do what is best for me. It was time to grow and change. I stopped trying to please everyone else. I feel SO comfortable in this new position. I am glad I listened to me. It even resulted in an increase in my compensation.

Now that you can see more clearly, what advice would you offer to other women in the sisterhood?

First, listen to your gut. Talk to others for their insight but in the end, you are the one who has to live with your decision. In your heart of hearts, you know what is right for you. Listen to yourself.

Anything else?

I would also tell them don't be afraid to have crazy ideas. Shift your perspective. Choose to worry less about what others will think of you and focus on what is needed. The rest will fall into place.

#theJalilastory   #myJalila

JALILA

INSPIRATION ON THE JOURNEY TO FREEDOM

Affirmations

A powerful tool to reinforce your conscious desire to shift the way you think . . .

> *It's up to me to articulate my value.*
>
> *I choose to own the power I DO have.*
>
> *It is no one else's job to stand up for me. I have the strength to stand up for myself.*
>
> *The world will value me when I value myself.*
>
> *I have the strength to be my biggest advocate.*

Songs to Motivate You

"Independent Woman" Pt 1 by Destiny's Child

"RESPECT" by Aretha Franklin

"Just Fine" by Mary J Blige

"Not a Pretty Girl" by Ani Difranco

Movies/Books to Energize You:

Legally Blonde

I Am Malala . . . Was Shot by the Taliban

True Stories to Energize You

GreatBigStory.com – Search "High Fashion's Hijab Queen"

GreatBigStory.com – Search "Claressa – Fighting to Stay on Top"

The Nikki Story

I'M OKAY IN THE BACKGROUND

Nikki, a mid-level career executive, was identified as a high potential employee for one of the world's most well-known brands with hundreds of thousands of staff worldwide. She had moved up in operations, had a knack for complex assignments, and was known for challenging the status quo. Nikki knew that it would probably be another five years before she could go after a senior level executive position. She was paying her dues and following a rather predictable path laid out before her. She was having some success – she had cracked the six-figure mark - but no matter how hard she worked, things were not moving as fast as she had hoped. (Sound familiar?)

She knew there had to be a better, faster way to grow her professional success, but how? Maybe her confidence level was holding her back. Maybe it was her presentations skills. Surely there was SOMETHING she could do, right?

In the meantime, she was working on a specific goal: to present to an audience of one hundred people without being nervous. For some reason, she could not find the confidence to do so. Nikki had talent, knowledge, technical skills and savvy to influence others one on one. However, she kept tripping up on confidence issue. That's when she reached out to me.

As I helped her polish her presentation, we talked about the bigger picture. "Kim, I want to be in that senior level position," Nikki said. "I'll do whatever it takes to be ready." With that statement, everything shifted - we went from working on Nikki's presentation to building her leadership brand.

We carefully examined every single signal she was sending out in her professional world. One seemingly minor detail we decided to change was her professional headshot. As we reviewed the details of her upcoming photo shoot, I asked Nikki what she planned to wear. "Perhaps you could wear a red jacket," I suggested, thinking the color would look striking against her dark olive skin.

"No! I cannot do that," she quickly retorted. We went through the rest of our session together in silence. As we wrapped up, I decided to give the topic one more try.

"Nikki, would you consider wearing a red jacket for the shoot?"

She began to frown and reject the idea again, but as she opened her mouth, all that came out was a startled, quiet, "Oh no!" She quickly placed her hand over her mouth and her eyes grew huge. "I just realized why I can't wear a red jacket. Both my parents are from India. In the town they came from, the bride wears red so that all eyes are on her. I can't wear red because I don't want all eyes on me." Tears began to fall on her cheeks. "How am I going to reach that senior executive level if I'm not comfortable with all eyes being on me?"

The "red jacket moment" played a pivotal role in Nikki's transformation. It completely shifted her perspective. Nikki continued to give everything she had to her company, investing blood, sweat and tears, but her company could not, would not, catch up with her growth. Within eighteen months, she was recruited to be a high-level DIRECTOR for a major corporation. They paid for her to relocate her family, she increased her salary by 51%, and most importantly, **she stepped into her power** with such momentum, there was –and is - no stopping her.

The last time I heard from Nikki was in the form of a text, sent from her private corporate jet: "I could get used to living like this!"

Here is a key part of the story that even I did not know until she shared it recently.

"And to think, none of this would have happened if I did not fight – and I mean *fight* - for the company to invest in me through executive coaching. I had to ask not once, but twice, before they agreed to it. Where would I be if I had given up?"

Did you hear that? **She is the one who asked** that the company invest in her. And she did not stop until it happened. What a legacy she is creating for her daughters!

I'm okay in the background	▶	I AM powerful and that's okay	▶	My power is MUCH needed in this world

LIFE WITH NIKKI IN THE RED ZONE

"I'm okay in the background."

When someone is in the red zone with Nikki, these are the kinds of things you will hear:

- "I don't know why I can't find the confidence."
- "I think it is more important to focus on my team."
- "I don't need to be out front. Really. . . it's ok."
- "I just want to serve/take care of the others."

This is the energy behind Nikki in the red zone. Keep in mind it is often unspoken. You have to pause and look closely to realize what is going on.

- Hidden
- Shy
- Uncertain
- Low self-importance
- Trapped
- Frightened

- Timid or doubtful
- Hesitant to shine
- Confined by expectations
- Pinned down
- Rule bound

LOOKING FARTHER DOWN THE ROAD

When we spend time with Nikki in the red zone, here are some of the unintended consequences:

- **It's all about everyone one else** - The red zone of Nikki takes the idea of being selfless to the extreme. The question is why? You deserve as much respect, love and honor as everyone else.

- **Staying in the background – consciously or not – sometimes hides another issue.** The red zone of Nikki can often mask Kari's expectation for perfection. If deep down we believe the world has deemed us as not measuring up in some way (looks, status, intelligence, etc.), it is quite possible we have learned to hide. It would be helpful to remember Kari's green zone: "I am enough."

- **We unconsciously absorb messages about "our place" in the world** – Is it possible we are teaching our daughters and sons that women should be seen, not heard? For our daughters, this translates into missed opportunities throughout life – from the way we introduce ourselves with impact to how we negotiate salaries. The underlying message shows up in our personal world too.

- **Our relationship with power becomes distorted** - Too often women unconsciously equate power with control. Far too many of us have experienced the controlling side of others. Even more have dealt with unsafe environments – emotionally and/or physically. The opportunity lies in women re-establishing a new, healthy relationship with the essence of power.

LIFE IN THE GREEN ZONE

"My power is much needed in this world."

When someone is in the green zone with Nikki, here are the kinds of things you will hear:

- "I can do this."

- "I can't believe I waited so long!"

- "There is no holding back now."

- "I feel like a weight has been lifted off my shoulders."

- "Amazing what happens when you step into your power."

This is the energy behind Nikki living in the green zone. Keep in mind it is often unspoken; however, it radiates from the inside out. People notice, but they are not sure why.

- Propelled
- Full of love for self
- Done with doubt
- Fueled by a greater purpose
- Adventurer

- Clarity of purpose
- Soulful
- Calmly confident
- Non-apologetic
- Poised and purposeful
- Genuine

Never doubt that a small group of thoughtful, committed ~~citizens~~ sisters can change the world; indeed, it's the only thing that ever has.

Margaret Mead

THE REST OF THE STORY: A FOLLOW-UP CONVERSATION WITH NIKKI

Can you describe the ah-ha moment for you?

The red-jacket moment. It hit on all the subconscious issues. Once we addressed those, I felt the break-through. The shackles holding me back were removed.

What was it like to realize your biggest obstacle was an internal mindset?

It was like a veil had been lifted and I could see clearly. I also knew that since it was internal, I was in control and could change it. It would take time but it was within my power to change. It was a choice I would have to make.

What did it feel like to you inside to rewire that thought process? How did it FEEL to take that action to move you to where you are today?

It was exciting and scary at the same time. Knowing I was in charge was great, but it also presented me with closed doors I wasn't sure I wanted to open. I had some self-doubt initially that I had to overcome. I was apprehensive at first, a bit overwhelmed by my power. I had to become comfortable in this "new skin." I am still amazed by it, and I don't take a minute of it for granted. I still have to remind myself and sometimes I falter. Every day I feel stronger.

What did it feel like when you started to step into that personal power? What might it look like to someone who might still be stuck?

> *It felt like I was taking ownership and accountability, which can be scary because this is new territory. I was stuck in the narrative I had defined myself and on some level it was "comfortable" there. In that world, I knew the "rules." This evolved version of myself was like a trust exercise with myself. I was depending on me to catch it when I took a misstep. When I saw myself going back to my old ways, I would call it out mentally and pivot. For example, I would sometimes display behaviors of a role one level down and I would catch myself. It felt comfortable because it was familiar, but that's not my role anymore.*

The happiness and shock in your voice when you told me about the 51% increase was amazing. You shared your excitement of spreading the message to other women so they could change their lives too. Why is that important?

> *I have taken three mentees "under my wing." With all three of them, I was recommended to them as a mentor. A great feeling and honor. One of the mentees said she was so nervous to meet me because of my title but she felt completely comfortable talking with me when we met . . . I was a "real" person. That comment made me laugh because I don't see myself based on my title, but it showed me the lenses other people see me through . . . how times have changed.*

Mentoring these three has been a wonderful experience . . . seeing them grow and enabling them to reach their best self is a gift. This is how we can change the Narrative and support one another. It doesn't mean we have to agree with one another, but it does mean we help one another.

Men learn this from an early age when they play games *. . . in football, the quarterback calls the plays and all help him. Men may not agree, but they do not display it publicly . . . they discuss in private, and help each other. Women do not learn this because we play different games . . . ones of fairness and niceness, which do nothing to prepare us for the real world.*

In light of what you have learned on your journey over the past few years, what is the biggest lesson you hope to teach your two daughters?

> **Don't let yourself get in the way of your greatness.** *The only thing stopping them from reaching their goal is themselves. They are each other's best friends and biggest supporters. They MUST always help one another achieve the best version of themselves.*

ONE FINAL THOUGHT

As Nikki's story continues, so do the lessons she learns and shares with us.

Shortly after her 'red jacket moment,' Nikki decided to go after a stretch assignment but faced a new stumbling block: pushback from her female boss, who didn't believe Nikki was ready. It was a variation of Avalene's red zone - *"I'm not qualified enough*"- coming to life. Nikki was startled by the pushback from someone she had viewed as an advocate for women.

Instead of backing down to her boss and away from her newfound power, Nikki stood strong. She remained calmly confident, calmly passionate. After an in-depth discussion with her boss, Nikki sent this email to her boss as a follow-up:

> *I realized after I hung up that I may have sounded like I was not comprehending or listening to your message about expectations. I want to reassure you that I do fully understand what you are saying and my expectations are not over-inflated. I want to be considered for these positions based on my merits and performance. Studies have shown that men will apply to jobs when they only meet 60% of the qualifications but women only apply when they meet 100% of the qualifications. I do not want to be part of that statistic. Even if I do not get the job, I will have gained interview experience, made additional connections, and received greater exposure . . . these are all positives that will help me define my career path.*

Wow – brave move. When she showed me the email, even I was inspired by Nikki's transformation. Nikki, however, was still truly baffled by her boss's behavior. *Why would Jennie have such a hard time with my request?* she kept asking herself. The answer is in the DNA of Jennie's thoughts - thoughts that were rooted in his-story and had been passed down through the generations.

Nikki's boss Jennie was sixty-three. The system was very different when she moved up the ranks. When she started at the company thirty years ago, working women were an anomaly.

There were very few women anywhere in the corporate ranks. She learned to act like one of the guys and never show vulnerability. She was rewarded for her toughness. Her southern charm had served her well while covering up a "make it happen" fortitude. She grew up professionally when the rule book was different for men and women: no questions asked. And now that she was close to retirement, her decades of determination were finally paying off. Following the rules had gotten her this far and she was not about to mess it up now. Jennie's experience was very different than Nikki's. Jennie herself was <u>unaware</u> that she was trapped by the red zone of the Sisterhood.

Nikki's quest for her personal power has something to teach us all. Instead of dealing with the situation from a victimhood mentality (no one supports women moving up) or with a sledgehammer (I will show her!), Nikki was <u>calmly confident, calmly passionate</u>. She created her new reality one small step at a time.

The take-a-way for each of us? Have compassion for those who came before you. Ask Judgment to step aside. Look at what is happening in terms of *the collective narrative*. It will shed light on the situation. Understand she (Jennie, in this case) is likely still in the fishbowl. Maybe you will be the instrument to inspire her to 'see' differently. Unlike you, she had no choice but to survive in a world driven by his-story. And above all, remember she is a sister too.

#theNikkistory   #myNikki

NIKKI

INSPIRATION ON THE JOURNEY TO FREEDOM

Affirmations

A powerful tool to reinforce your conscious desire to shift the way you think . . .

I was not made to stand in the shadows.

Power is not a bad word.

Power and beauty are not mutually exclusive.

This world needs me!

It's okay for me to shine.

Songs to Motivate You

"This Is for My Girls" by Michelle Obama

"Run the World" by Beyonce

"Fight Song" by Rachel Platten

"Unwritten" by Natasha Bedingfield

"Superwoman" by Alicia Keys

Movies & Books to Energize You:

Wonder Woman

The Post

Hunger Games

True Stories to Inspire You:

GreatBigStory.com – Search "A Field Between"

Youtube.com – Search "The Greatest Showman | "This Is Me" with Keala Settle" (the story behind the making of the movie)

GreatBigStory.com – Search "The Army of Moms Standing Up"

GreatBigStory.com – Search "A Café Run by Heroes"

How the Sisters Come to Life

Now that you've met each sister, it's time to take a step back and look at the big picture: the Sisterhood as a whole.

Download the inspiration guide at YourLionInside.com of all their mindsets – a one-page sisterhood you can print and keep with you. Use it as an inspiration to bring out the best of the Sisterhood in your life.

Remember this is a continuum, one step at a time. Small actions have BIG impact. Simply start with the sister who resonates with you the most. The rest will fall into place.

Keep coming back until these seven mindsets are rooted in your psyche, until you no longer have to consciously choose the empowering mindsets, until they have become part of your subconscious.

The Sisterhood is for sharing, so I encourage you to share these mindsets with any woman you believe could benefit from discovering her own lion inside. If there is one thing we can all agree on, it's that we can often see in each other what we can't see in ourselves.

HOW THE SISTERS *REALLY* SHOW UP

"Everyone realizes that these mindsets don't show up in life in nice neat red, yellow and green zones like this, right?" Darsha asks.

Jalila nods. "It is important to look for the subtleties of how the red mindsets work, what they look like."

"It would be helpful to hear some examples of how these mindsets weave themselves into everyday life," Kari says.

Thank you, Kari. That is exactly where we are heading . . .

IN THE EYES OF A 5-YEAR-OLD

In November of 2015, I attended a publishing conference sponsored by Hay House in Orlando with Reid Tracy, editor of Hay House, and *New York Times* bestselling author Cheryl Richardson. Throughout the conference, participants were asked to stand up and share their story. One of those volunteers was a woman named Angela. To this day, she does not know she impacted the development of this book.

"I am a consultant who travels around the country and I recently learned that my five-year-old daughter needs to have four molars removed," Angela began. "As we rode home from the dentist, my daughter asked me an innocent question. 'Mom, will the tooth fairy be visiting me when the molars come out?' In my head I thought no, the tooth fairy comes only when teeth fall out naturally. I told her I would check and let her know. Later than night, as I was talking about it with my husband, I realized I was really bothered by her request. It was against "the rules." *(This is Kari's red zone showing up. Breaking the rules would not fit the image of perfection.)* The tooth fairy only comes when teeth fall out."

"I did not understand why I was struggling with her simple request. After all, we were talking about *the tooth fairy*! She was made up, with rules that were also made up, right? I slept on it. The next day, I remembered an article I read in *Forbes* magazine about how women are 33% less likely to ask for what they want. This was one of many reasons women have trouble later in their careers negotiating the salary they desire. When I connected the dots, I decided if my 5-year-old daughter had the guts to ask, the tooth fairy would deliver! Who was I to stand in the way of my daughter's attempt to rewrite the story?"

A powerful yet simple reminder to pay attention to opportunities that allow our daughters to think differently.

THE SISTERHOOD IS DIFFERENT FOR EACH OF US

While the Sisterhood of Seven is an important part of all our journeys, know that your experience with the sisters is yours alone – and it will be constantly changing. Perhaps you will relate to Flora's story.

I met Flora, the little cousin of one of my closest friends, when she was 28 years old, living on the outskirts of San Francisco. She did not come to me looking for help; I happened to come into her life and offered to help. I could see so much in her that she could not see in herself. Vivacious and full of energy, Flora was a delight to be around. However, whenever the conversation turned to her professional life, it was as if a blanket had been thrown over her, suddenly blocking out all light. I could actually see her energy wane as we talked about her career. She would shuffle uncomfortably, explaining she had a condition that impacted her ability to work. Obviously, this was not a subject she wanted to talk about. So instead, I would ask about her professional dreams. Flora had no answer; she did not allow herself to dream. She had resigned herself to her lot in life and had split her world in half. *At work I am one person, everywhere else I am another*. I was baffled - this was a bright, talented, intelligent, outgoing young woman. If she felt defeated at 28, what went through her mind when she thought about the rest of her life?

One afternoon, I had a chance to meet Flora's mother, Anna. When we had a few moments alone, her mom shared more.

"In fifth grade, Flora was diagnosed with central auditory processing disorder, CAPD for short. Basically, it meant she needed more time to process information and needed things in writing. Hearing the information did not connect for her," Anna explained. "Flora had to have a special assistant through-out school to take notes for her. There were resources for her in middle school, which helped. In high school there was no help, so she really struggled. When it came time for college, we actively sought a school that had resources for her, and she did really, really well. In fact, she even had a better GPA than her siblings. What Flora always had was conscientiousness. I have never seen someone work so hard."

When I started coaching Flora, it soon became evident she was living in the red zone of many of the sisters. She was also hanging out with Fear and Powerlessness, who were waving disability in front of Flora's face like a surrender flag. I could see so much potential in Flora, but she could not see it for herself. Her "disability" was blinding her to possibilities. The ah-ha came when we redefined the way she saw her disability. Remember, pause – reflect – choose.

"Flora, why are you allowing CAPD to define you? Has it ever occurred to you the hard work you put in to overcome it is exactly why you are good at what you do?" I asked.

It took that one question for her to shift her perspective. And that shifted everything, putting into motion a complete transformation. The rest of the story is best heard from Flora herself.

Why did you allow a disability to stand in your way professionally?

> Because I was afraid that if I admitted to others that some crucial aspect of my job as an assistant - such as listening and taking verbal instruction - wasn't something I excelled at, people would automatically shut me down for a position.

What did it feel like inside to rewire the way you thought about CAPD? It was a pretty big ah-ha moment when you started to see it as positive instead of negative. You said it triggered something in you.

> People tend to hear "learning disability" as a negative. It was hard as a student growing up to feel like I wasn't a failure based on the title I was associated with. When I first met Kim, I was very stand-offish about what I wanted others to perceive. If I let someone know that I had this disability, then it would be like admitting defeat all over again. (Do you hear Kari's red zone speaking here?) I felt like it would automatically take me out of the level playing field with the rest of the world. By the second time we talked, I started to realize that someone who had never met me didn't see the "negative" CAPD. Kim actually saw that it was something that made me a great executive assistant. It made me wonder if other people could see the same thing. It took an outsider to tell me that my value didn't lie within an associated negative title. My value is within all

the struggle and perseverance I put in to get past it. That is what makes me so good at what I do.

Each time you went on an interview, you got stronger and stronger. What does that look like to someone who might still be stuck?

The first interview I went into, I felt totally defeated. I felt like I was totally unqualified (Avalene's red zone). I was convinced they would never see my assets. When they asked me questions, I sometimes couldn't remember the question due to the CAPD! It was extremely frustrating. Once I got the hang of what the interview questions were and what to expect, I could put all my tools to good use. By that I mean, I could be confident in my answers and then I could simply be myself the rest of the way through. It was really a matter of saying to myself, "Do the best you can. Keep a positive attitude, even when you flub up." That goes a long way as I can only be me at the end of the day — I am fairly sure this was the Sisterhood talking - ha!

The moment I felt a real sense of personal power was when I started receiving multiple follow-up interviews. I realized these people saw value in all that I was as an assistant and all that I was as a person (moving into Kari's green zone here). Those two things were more powerful than my disability could ever be.

Flora, you mentioned I didn't allow you to make any excuses. Why was that important?

You never let me think I can't do that or say that to them because it'll tell them I'm faulty! I wrote in my notebook my biggest asset is being detail-oriented because I have no other option. That was HUGE! Simply hearing someone on the outside say, "Perhaps you're bigger than you think you are," when it isn't ever something you have believed, is a game-changer. I really was living small like a kitten when I had the strength of a lion inside.

You learned to have the faith that what was meant to happen, would. Why was that important and how was that different from before?

I've always lived my life with the mentality that if something is right, it'll fall into place. When I had multiple interviews with many companies and not one resulted in a job offer, I figured I was meant to stay at my humdrum job. I gave up thinking there was anything better.

After I recognized the Sisterhood, I saw things differently. I had more confidence. When one company told me, after three rounds of interviews, that I wouldn't be getting the job, an odd sense of calmness came over me. I had faith that if I kept interviewing with more companies, I'd find a fit that was right for everyone. Rushing never gets you anywhere but into a mistake, right? With my newfound confidence, I didn't want the "right now" job; I wanted the "right fit" job. It was never that I wasn't good enough for the job; the companies and I were not compatible on all levels. I wasn't a failure, I simply wasn't a fit. And when I

> *found the right fit, my salary package was 35% more than it would have been at the "wrong fit" job. All because I finally learned to see things differently.*

Since then, you've been so excited about encouraging other women. Why?

> *I've always been a pretty encouraging and positive person. My old coworker was the complete opposite. It drove me nuts. It also discouraged me personally, thinking perhaps this was the best thing out there. Once I realized there are GREAT companies who value their employees -and whose employees value each other - it solidified that my positive energy wasn't misplaced. It was right at home in my new position.*
>
> *At some point, I think we all get stuck in the mindsets of those around us. We limit ourselves by others' negativity. Their own personal limitations become ours. Having a place and people who openly appreciate you for who you are as a person is empowering and energizing. It is truly impossible to not want to share and encourage others to find a place that is their "right fit."*

THE SISTERHOOD SHOWS UP
WHEN YOU LEAST EXPECT IT

Gabriella is my girl, the sister I am closest to. I call her Gabi. Of all the sisters, she is the one who stays nearest to me. "*I got your back girl,*" she says. She has wiped my tears away on many occasions. She has cheered me on when I faced challenges. Even as I was in the final stages of writing this book, Gabi reminded me of what is truly being asked by us all: to "see" things differently in our professional and *personal* lives. The Sisterhood is not limited to work. They show up at home too.

I unexpectedly married again two years ago. No one was more surprised than I when "never" came knocking at my door. I was blessed with a man who was able to break through my tough exterior and touch the depths of my heart. Our blended families included my daughter Heather, his two daughters, his son, granddaughters and great granddaughters. For the first time in my life, I learned from him what unconditional love really means. It was in this heart space I blossomed. *I was finally safe.* Peter is much older than me, but he remains young in spirit. Still, it was not an easy decision to go down this path with him, knowing time was especially precious for us. However, it was in this safe zone that my husband helped me dissect the messages many women internalize by showing me *how it happens.* He has endured my requests to view our life like a sitcom. I would carefully request emotion be removed from the situation and to lovingly help me discover how a sister shows up. That would be the case with the appearance of Gabi.

It began with a simple discussion about cars. I have a Jeep Wrangler and we've shared many laughs over my rebellious choice in cars. It was the first car I ever purchased on my own. Despite deep affection for my adventurous pal, there was one other car that would stop me in my tracks. Every. Single. Time. I would drool as she drove by. I would sigh with longing when I saw her parked. My daughter said it was the one thing I have ever said I actually wanted out loud. My husband discovered this. "We should find a used one," he said. I was in shock! "Are you kidding me?" was my reply. Little did I know, Gabi was along for this ride.

On Monday, the day of the infamous 2017 solar eclipse visible in the US, my husband heard about a used model for sale. We decided to go for a test drive - and viewed one of the most important celestial events of the century at a car dealership. I had great fun test-driving the car. It was like stepping into a dream. I never had the courage to ever test it out in the real world. Subconsciously, I had filed it away in the wistful *someday when I win the lottery* mental folder. The model we test drove had everything we were looking for – price, mileage, care, etc. Except I was not excited about the color - a rich chocolate brown with a camel interior. Keep in mind, back in my dream world, just *thinking* about this car would bring me to tears. But here I was standing beside one, and there was nothing - no feeling at all. I kept waffling back and forth as I discussed it with my husband. I said I wanted to call my daughter Heather.

My desire to "phone a friend" sparked an intense discussion right there in the parking lot. "You need to learn to think on your own," he stated with conviction. "Why do you need other people's opinion? Why don't you trust your own opinion?"

Valid point. Something I need to work on, check.

He told me that choosing a car is a very personal decision, based on taste. Deep down, I was torn. I wanted to like the car, but I was feeling hesitant about the color. Earlier, he had jokingly asked, "What is it about women and colors of cars – geez?"

Now, I knew *he* liked the color. Despite not liking the color, I could feel myself wanting to please him. I was also paralyzed by the fear of making the wrong decision – again. Can you

relate? Deep down, unconsciously, I guess I wanted his approval – even though I was forty eight years old. *Ugh Gabi – I
thought we made peace with this sista!* Evidently, Gabi and I
had some work to do.

Two days later, I found the car I LOVED at a dealer two
hundred miles away. I adored the beautiful deep blue exterior
and the gorgeous creamy interior. It fit the mileage specs, was
inexpensive to transport and had been well cared for. And. .
.it made me cry! I could not wait to show my husband. When
he came home, he quickly looked at the website on his phone
and casually mentioned the car was not a color he cared for.
Without much thought, it appeared he had dismissed it, mum-
bling something about looking at it later, and he left.

I was crushed. It felt like ice water had been dumped all over
me. I was surprised by how I felt in that moment. Powerless.
Through my journey with the sisters, I know with absolute cer-
tainty when I feel powerless, it is a trigger to figure out what is
not right. *"What is going on, Kimberly?"* I asked myself.

An hour later, Peter called to suggest I look at another
used car. I quietly internalized the unspoken message (or so
I thought) - *Keep looking. The choice you made this morning
was not a good one.* By now, I really did not like how I was feeling. I was baffled. *Why did he dismiss what I wanted? He just
told me Monday I need to think for myself. I tried to do that
today and yet I was dismissed. What message do I take away
from this now? Is this how these limiting mindsets internalize?*

I had a choice. I could choose to internalize that my opinion does not matter and feel my power erode just a bit. Or I
could address it head on. Remember the self-fulfilling prophecy and confirmation bias? The outcome would be predictable
based on which side of Gabi I chose.

My beloved came home later in the day. I asked if we could have an objective conversation about the car experience - like we were watching a sitcom. He agreed. I showed him the one page sisterhood outline and explained how I was wrestling with Gabi. I felt like the red side of Gabi was winning. I was trying to trust my own opinion but I was baffled about how the car process was unfolding.

Amused but committed, he processed the entire experience with me – *for the benefit of the book* he said. He explained his thought process: he questioned the logistics of purchasing a car so far away, was it worth the effort, what could go wrong – all unspoken. He could now see how I might have perceived his silence as not having confidence in my opinion. I told him how thankful I was to be able to have this conversation. "Wow, to think how close I was to not bringing this up," I said. "I would have walked away with perceptions that would have kept me stuck with Gabi's red zone."

In response, he offered these nuggets of wisdom:

"Two important things to remember, Kim," he said. "First, women often don't voice those misperceptions. Many times us guys are not even given a chance to correct it." I agreed and he continued. "Second, I understand how you were not able to test assumptions like these with men – personally and professionally - earlier in your life. Thank goodness you feel *safe* enough now to see things differently." I nodded in gratitude as he leaned over to kiss me.

"This conversation is so important to the book, Peter. Women can learn how this process unfolds so we catch it. Only then is there a chance for change. Only then can we teach our daughters to think differently," I said. "My struggle with

Gabriella's mindset is a big life challenge. This mindset of seeking approval has been a major roadblock in my life."

He paused and lovingly said, "You know how many times we have laughed about why our girl Heather calls so often asking for your advice about what to do? Perhaps she learned it from her mama." Wow. Reality check.

WHAT I COULD NOT 'SEE'

My mind spinning, I went back to work on the final stages of the book. *Is this how it happens? Is this how we internalize beliefs which do not serve us or our daughters? Do we really see the world so differently that, instead of testing our assumptions, we simply accept what is not said out loud? Then the silent messages play out day by day.* But something was missing. Then it hit me.

FEAR.

At the core of my seeking permission and approval was Fear – yet another mean girl of our mindset. Fear loves to remind me of the times I have not made good decisions. Fear makes me wonder if I might screw things up again.

Is Fear interfering with the entire sisterhood? Decide for yourself –

- Is Kari's search for *perfection* masking a deep-seated fear of not being enough?
- Is Ranee's desire to *meet everyone's needs* driven by the fear of letting someone down? Fear of not giving enough?
- Is Gabi's *need for permission or approval* rooted in fear of disappointing someone? Not living up to expectations?

- Is Darsha's need to *accept what is said* simply a cover for fear of judgment, fear of being wrong or fear of making yet another mistake?

- Was Avalene's thought of *not being qualified enough* simply an attempt to avoid potential disappointment? Deep down, was she hanging out with Kari, fearful of not being enough?

- Surely, Jalila's desire to *work hard and be rewarded* is pure. Or is she also hiding a deeply rooted fear of not <u>having</u> enough, <u>being</u> enough or <u>doing</u> enough?

- Nikki's desire to *stay in the background* can't be rooted in fear, or can it? What is Nikki afraid of? Is she trying to avoid being rejected? Is she scared someone will discover she is not perfect along with her sister Kari? Or is she fearful that her light will shine so bright that the sheer magnitude of her fullness could actually make a difference in the world?

Each of us will have to answer these questions for ourselves. One thing is for certain: the red side of all the sisters begins with Kari's quest for perfection. It ends with her deep, profound acceptance of *I am enough*. Deep down, Kari's story is *our* story.

It really is a circle - no beginning, no end. Each mindset connected like a web.

If we stay close to the red mindsets of the Sisterhood – or continue to ignore what is happening before our very eyes, it will keep us spinning. Predictably, in a downward spiral.

If, however, we courageously and <u>consciously</u> choose to live life from the green side of the Sisterhood, then we grow into the fullest version of who we are. We will continue to move in a circle, yes. But this time, it will spin in an upward direction propelling us up and forward.

Day by day, decision by decision, we have a choice. What will you choose?

THE POWER OF INTENTION

Before you read this section, close your eyes and take three long, deep, slow breaths. When we take the time to breathe slowly, we send a signal to our bodies that we are safe which opens a channel to hear ourselves with more clarity. Clear your mind and ask yourself honestly which sister(s) resonates with you. Keep her in mind as you read this section.

Intention is the energy behind the "why" we are doing something. Your intention is the unspoken need behind your choice. Two people can take the same action; however, for one person, it is *not* the right thing and for the other person it is. Intention is a small, subtle difference that is *everything* – and it's why so many of us are confused about the messages we receive in the world.

For example: hosting a wedding shower. For one woman, it is an opportunity to plan an incredible celebration and un-leash her creativity as an expression of who she is. She's not doing it to impress people - it brings her great satisfaction. You can see her beaming and the joy radiates from the inside out. To another woman, however, throwing a wedding shower is an expected, burdensome task. The responsibility, the plan-ning and the effort involved takes such a personal toll that the energy behind the party is draining.

For me, as someone who has battled an eating disorder, intention comes to life with something as simple as a piece of chocolate. If I am eating a piece of chocolate because I want to enjoy it, that is fine and healthy. However, if I am eating the same piece of chocolate to fill a void inside – to unconsciously calm an emotion I can't quite recognize or don't want to deal with - then that is something else entirely. Looks the same to the outside world, with a very different meaning on the inside.

Intention matters even when we are drawn to purchase something. It doesn't matter if it is a handbag, a designer dress, plastic surgery or a car. The question - and the answer - is found in asking *why*. Why are you purchasing this? Simply because you want to enjoy it? Or are you buying it to meet an ego need or fill an emptiness inside yourself? Therein lies a huge myth perpetuated by many in the world. Let me remind you there is nothing you can purchase that will <u>make you matter</u> more than you do right now.

Many of us are facing – or soon will face - the pressures of caring for an ailing family member. It could be a disabled child, a spouse with an illness or aging parents. Extreme situations like these are never easy. Many caregivers feel guilty for asking for help. They feel they "should" be the primary caretaker. This is the Narrative, once again. Add the red mindset of Ranee (I have to meet all demands) and Kari (I expect perfection), and you're on the fast track to the crazy house. It is okay to love yourself enough to draw boundaries. It is okay to ask for help. Instead of caving into guilt, ask yourself honestly *why* you are seeking help. If it is because you genuinely can't handle it anymore and it is taking a toll on your health, know that it is ok. The power lies in the intention behind it. **Deeply understanding the intention behind the mindset holds the key to the freedom you desire.**

Some people have wondered why "Sisterhood" is not part of the title of this book. The answer is simple: the real message here is about unleashing the power that's already inside you. The Sisterhood is but one way to do that, to shift from living life with the smallness of a meow to the strength of a roar. Living small serves no one.

The Sisterhood is a loving way for each of us to "see" the world differently. To think differently. To live differently. To encourage our sisters – above, beside and below us - to do the same. One hundred years from now, when our sisters are taking up the next chapter of empowerment, the Sisterhood they know may be different. But the core message of power, freedom and love is timeless.

IN THE EYES OF A 102-YEAR-OLD

Despite the fact that my mother-in-law Rose has lived 27,856,800 more minutes than I have, even a 102-year-old is acquainted with the Sisterhood. Many weeks ago, she was dancing with Drama right next to Tizzy. It was quite a sight! When asked what was wrong, she explained with much angst how she was having trouble grooming in the morning. Her hands could no longer hold the mirror and the comb. It was exhausting and she was feeling quite sorry for herself, allowing Victimhood to overstay her welcome.

"Rose, I can easily take care of that," I said. "Why haven't you told us before now?" After much explanation, I finally realized that the red zone of Kari (*I expect perfection)* and Ranee (*I have to meet all demands*) had been doing their thing.

It took me less than twenty-four hours to address the mirror and comb issue. Rose was shocked. "Was it really that easy?" she asked. It was hard for her to accept that yes, it really was that easy.

So I shared a <u>mantra</u> with her. "Repeat after me, Rose," I began.

"Life . . .

Does not . . .

Have to be . . .

So hard!"

She smiled and Laughter graced us with her presence. Keep Rose's mantra close to heart.

The Sisterhood Mourns a Loss

"Kari, is it hard for you when we talk to someone new about the Sisterhood?" Jalila asks.

"You mean does it make me think about Kailyn?" Kari half-smiles. "Of course it does, and that's okay. I think about my twin every day. No matter what."

"I know, sweetie," Nikki says, wrapping an arm around Kari. "We all miss Kailyn."

"Our lost sister," Ranee says. "A part of each of us died with her."

"She had *so much* to offer," Gabi shakes her head. "But her quest for perfection consumed her."

"Until it killed her," Kari says flatly.

"She missed all the signs," Avalene says. "So many people tried to save her."

"We *all* tried to save her," Nikki says.

"She could have saved *herself*. She had the power all along," says Kari. "She chose not to believe it."

The Sisterhood's message is bigger than improving your station in life. Sometimes, it is as basic and important as saving your life.

Dedicated to all the Kailyn's who leave us far too soon -

- To the Kailyn who endured an extremely toxic work environment for too many years. The stress eventually manifested into cancer of the brain. She thought if *I just work harder, I can turn things around.* RIP 59 years old.

- To the Kailyn who turned to alcohol and Xanax when the weight of being perfect was more than she could bear. She left behind three children and a confusing legacy for her daughters to unravel. RIP 46 years old.

- To the Kailyn who *still* believes she has to be the perfect daughter, the perfect girlfriend, the perfect boss. A tumor has already shown up – a red light, a warning to stop. But she doesn't – *she thinks she can't* – take the warning seriously and continues her quest for perfection. Every day she is offered a choice to embrace the profound truth of "I am enough." If she doesn't, we know what will happen. This Kailyn is only 32 years old.

"There is always a choice. Love yourself enough," the Sisterhood reminds us all.

Before I Knew the Sisterhood

I came close to becoming another Kailyn.

Long before I knew the Sisterhood, I was fighting for survival, only I didn't realize it at the time. I was very busy trying to make sense of this thing called life. It wasn't turning out quite how I had envisioned it as a little girl. Why didn't finding Prince Charming make it all better? The movies I had watched said it would be okay then. Happily ever after was the Holy Grail. Had I taken a wrong turn? Was something wrong with me? I was confused and bewildered. Then, I looked at the life of my mother. Why had she never found her Prince Charming? Was he not around in my grandmother's day either? Turning a blind eye to those questions, I was convinced if I kept pushing hard enough, I could make life turn out like it was supposed to.

After all, now that I had a daughter looking to me for leadership, the stakes were higher than ever. In 2002, I had earned partnership status with a nationally-known consulting firm with a clientele of many large corporations. The job required travel but the family pulled together to manage it. Year after year, my sweet girl was growing. By the time she was four, the realization that I would not have any more children of my own began to sink in. Every moment with my daughter became even more precious as a result.

I remember the day like it was yesterday: Heather was in the third grade and mornings had become a bit of a struggle. I would try to pull her hair back for school and she would refuse. *I am too cool for hair bows*, she would adamantly tell me. I searched for alternatives to the traditional hair bow. Back in those days, there were limited options. In my desperation to find an alternative that would bring peace to our mornings, I made a simple hair ornament with a ponytail holder and long ribbons. Heather loved it. She affectionately called them Sassytails – they made her feel sassy and they had tails. Voilá, our morning problem was solved. Little did I know what was to come.

As Heather wore these simple ornamental hair accessories, friends at school started to ask for them. My weekends became filled with assembling multiple accessories for her to share. Much to our surprise, other moms started to call and request these "darling accessories." Wherever Heather and I would travel, moms would stop us on the street asking us where to buy the product in Heather's hair. By the time a local cheer-leading squad requested an order, Heather was filled with ideas of her own. "*Mom, I have a great idea. We should start a business together and call it Sassytails*," she said going on to explain it would give us more time together so I would not have to travel so much. "*I will be vice president*," she declared.

Everyone told me I was crazy. *What a hair-brained idea!* they would declare, pun intended. *Why are you even considering it?* While I continued to work full-time, Heather and I started our small company, using our dining room table for the production line. By that point, I had started to recognize the messages the world was giving to girls about how they had to look and act a certain way. I had heard similar messages growing up, but now my daughter's future was at stake. It made me see the world differently. I did the research and over $50 million worth of ponytail holders per year were sold in the US alone. Suddenly, I began to really wonder if there was something to this idea. Was it possible to create a company that could inspire girls to realize they were beautiful the way they were? Could Heather and I set an example for others that girls could create a very different future than what was expected?

In the summer of 2004, we tested the concept at a kiosk in Myrtle Beach, South Carolina. I figured the test market would allow Heather and I time together while inspiring her to dream big. I also thought it would show that the idea did not have enough merit to move forward. Boy, was I wrong! We discovered that moms from all over the country were evidently having the same issue. People were inspired by a seven-year-old vice president and mother-daughter entrepreneur team. By the end of the summer, I boldly took the leap. I knew this was going to be my only child, and I was determined to show her dreams can come true.

In 2004, we officially launched our company called Sassytails, fueled by a shared dream to change the way girls saw themselves and the world. Slowly, we grew from having our products sold in 20 stores and then 100 stores. Our products were in the Atlanta, Chicago, Dallas and Los Angeles showrooms. The story was compelling. As we grew, it became evident that the dream was taking on a life of its own. I started to seek investors so we could scale the dream and broaden our reach. Keep in mind the internet was in its infancy back then. The only way to grow was to sell product to retailers. Trade show after trade show, the interest and orders grew. My quest for investors became critical as it became clear that it would take a while for the profitability to scale so I could take a salary. The deadline was set by the husband. Find investors by "x" or give up this crazy idea and find a real job with a steady paycheck. For months, I ran parallel tracks knowing time was running out. The pressure at home was mounting for a multitude of reasons. I would search for jobs in the morning and run Sassytails in the afternoon. I was baffled: I knew I could make a difference, but things were not happening fast enough. *Push harder,* I told myself. It came down to the last week of the deadline I was given. I had a follow-up interview with an agency for a job I was likely to be offered. My head said give up the dream and just take the job. My heart was crying for something very different. I scheduled my last opportunity for investors the same afternoon. My spirit torn, I knew I had come to the end of the road.

The morning of November 15, 2005 arrived. The 10:00 a.m. interview was with the board of directors of the agency. It went well and it became clear I was a good fit. The chairman of the board had not been able to attend at the last minute but the team assured me they would fill him in. I left the interview and listened to voicemails. More orders for Sassytails. My heart could barely stand it. *God, what do you want from me?* I asked.

The 3:00 p.m. investor meeting finally arrived. With heartfelt consideration, I gave it my all. I was supposed to meet with only one investor but he had unexpectedly invited another gentleman to attend. An hour and a half later, the meeting came to a close. Both men had daughters and were inspired by my vision to create a company that would positively impact girls. The second potential investor excused himself, saying he was due at an agency meeting - he had missed an important interview earlier that morning. We were able to put two and two together. He was the absent chairman of the board from my interview, and I was the important interview he had missed. "Oh-no," he said. "If we invest in Sassytails, you won't be able to take the job." The synchronicity surprised us all.

I drove home and waited. I said to the husband, whichever one comes through is a sign of the right path. At 6:00 p.m. the phone rang. It was the agency with a generous job offer. I said I would reply in the morning. Every ounce of my being was hoping for a different call. While the husband was relieved that this ridiculous business idea would soon be over, I continued to hold out hope. At 9:00 p.m., the phone rang again. It was the potential investors offering my full request for $300,000 to take Sassytails to the next level. I hung up and wept. Heather and I jumped for joy at our dream becoming a reality. I fought the Narrative being demanded of me. Nothing would stop us now. Or so I thought.

Fueled with an investment, momentum and enough passion to take on the world, our journey continued. I hired talented women who believed in our vision to support the growing demand. We grew to our products being sold to 400 stores, then 600 stores. Our ability to manufacture the product through our cottage network was no longer enough. We secured overseas manufacturing broadening our product line along the way. Heather led the creation of a junior advisory board, including the members in many of our business decisions. We were both deeply committed to creating a company *for* girls and *by* girls. We were on our way to building a brand that would positively influence the way girls see themselves and the world.

I could see the impact of being a vice president in the third grade was having on Heather's life. I still have the elementary collage of the things that were important to her. Right in the middle is her Sassytails business card. By that point, she had been part of product development, had worked our booth at trade shows and made presentations to investors. Despite what some people said, there was no telling Heather that she was vice president in name only. It changed her perspective of the world and made her believe she could do anything.

There's much more I could share about this amazing journey, but here are a few key accomplishments:

- We were able to secure a license with Warner Brothers for a line of Harry Potter accessories for girls. It was the most valuable consumer product license of the time. Our products were actually approved by J.K. Rowling's personal team. As a result of the license, we were invited to be guests on the red carpet at the Hollywood premiere of *The Order of the Phoenix*, and our products were even giveaways at the after party.

- The success with Warner Brothers opened the door to Disney working with us on licenses for the princesses, the fairies, High School Musical and others.

- We were in the process of raising an additional $3 million in capital to expand the brand internationally. A customized website was in development, so we could participate in a "growing trend" called *the internet*.

The entire Sassytails experience was a testament to the power of a vision. It was my first foray into creating my own path and learning to trust my own decisions. We all worked extremely hard and the learning curve was steep. I still faced numerous battles on the homefront, torn between doing what I was told I should do and doing what I knew I was *called* to do. Little did I know it was not wise to fight internal battles and external battles at the same time. I believed I was invincible. It turns out, I wasn't.

WHEN A DREAM BECOMES A NIGHTMARE

To this day, it is not easy for me to explain how it all came crashing down. The only way I can describe it is to say there was a perfect storm of circumstances. The success and level of growth was more than our small company could stand. Blinded by a dream, I was not able to see it at the time. A major investor had undiagnosed Alzheimer's, which led to decisions with serious implications. One of those decisions was involving a potential investor with malintent. For nine months, I desperately fought to save the company, but ended up a statistic of the economic crash of 2008. I was searching for change to buy a gallon of gas (a story I shared earlier in the book). The year ended with my declaring bankruptcy personally and professionally. Words cannot adequately express how heartbreaking it was to tell my very young vice president that sometimes dreams don't come true. My attempt to break free from the Narrative and create a new future turned into a nightmare.

I lost everything this world teaches us is important. Even more devastating, I lost my passion for life. I lost my belief in the goodness of people. I even stopped believing God was good. I gave up on my dreams and resigned myself to merely existing. I branded myself with a big "F" on my forehead: "F" for failure. I lost my confidence, the ability to trust my judgment and my desire to connect with other people. I did what I had to do to make it through each day, trying to be a mother to my precious girl.

My days were grey.

Years passed.

Shortly after Heather turned 12, she began asking me very tough questions - questions that were wise beyond her age. *Why are you doing that? Why do you put up with that? Why don't you stand up for what you really believe?* She would hold me accountable for why I said one thing and did another. Her insights and observations continued to such a degree that I was shocked at what I was *really* teaching my daughter. I had made a lot of progress, yes, but wow, I still had a long way to go.

As moms, we genuinely believe we are teaching our children the right lessons. We underestimate the impact of the incongruence of our messages. If our words say one thing but our actions say another, what do our daughters and sons really take away? When our actions and words are not in sync, there is a space – a confusing emptiness, a confusing chasm, a question not answered. When this happens over and over again, our children answer the question unconsciously, and it becomes part of their DNA of thought - it establishes certain patterns that significantly impact life moving forward. Remember the one-hundred-year-old narrative we started our journey with earlier in this book? How "old" mindsets are still tucked away in the DNA of our thoughts? Evidently, I had some tucked away too.

For me, Sassytails represented a chance to do something meaningful while claiming my independence. I had watched family members remain trapped by not having that independence which significantly limited their choices, and it frightened me. When my efforts failed, I came face to face with the belief that maybe the family had been right: life really is stacked against you, and you should just swallow the bitter pill and give up dreams of a better life. The DNA of thought that we are powerless to influence the outcome of our life was trying to kill my spirit. It seemed as if I was doomed to repeat history.

My mother, a stay-at-home mom for thirteen years, was catapulted unexpectedly into a work world for which she was not prepared. Scrambling to earn an associate's degree – proudly, I might add – she pressed on to figure out how to support herself and the family. The years following the divorce were frightening and traumatic for all involved. This "event," which happened when she was thirty-three years old – almost 35 years ago – still impacts her today as she faces retirement. It is a sobering reminder of cause and effect being far removed in space and time. I had a close-up view of the life of my mother, a fellow sister, driven by the mindsets of the generation before her. They taught her to believe someone would take care of her. They taught her to look outside of herself for the answers.

The experience drove me to vow *I will always be able to support myself.* This is a mental model, which has been a blessing and a curse in my life, as well as the life of my daughter. The challenges my mother and I had in our relationship were driven by a difference of perspective. Every time there was an emotional exchange, I was reminded of the importance of my work to shift the way I think so life would be different for my daughter.

For those of you who have faced numerous challenges growing up, perhaps you can relate. No picture-perfect family memories. There was little money for college education, much less advanced degrees. There were no opportunities without scratching and fighting for every cent. I vividly remember wanting to blame everyone else - God, society, social norms, family - for not providing opportunities others had. It took me a *long* time to learn that blame serves no one. I was at war with myself. I screamed at the heavens, *"I did not know better, dammit!"*

The divine answer I received was simple: *"You did not know then, but you do know <u>now.</u> Now is the only thing that matters. You have two choices, Kimberly: victimhood or victory. It is that simple. Despite the hardships and things out of your control, you also made choices that brought you to this place today. You can choose a new path. The cage you have placed yourself in has no back. Step out, dear one and live the life you were meant to live."*

I thought back to all the times I had second-guessed myself, said what I thought everyone else wanted to hear, and pushed deep down what I really needed. As agonizing as it was to accept, I had indeed played a role in my own disaster.

Even with the divine insight, I was paralyzed by fear. I was caught up in the shoulds, judgment of myself, and judgment from others. There were many well-meaning "religious" women who told me where my place was supposed to be. They frightened me of the huge mistakes I would make by leaving the marriage and changing my life. I came face to face with a major intersection of life: victimhood or victory, right? In 2011, I finally made the heartbreaking decision to move forward with a divorce. Having been paralyzed by the fact that I did not want to repeat the toxic divorce of my parents, it was life-changing to realize I could do it differently. I did not have to repeat the toxic patterns of the past. Determined to create a different experience, I did everything I could to move forward with compassion. I chose to leave with $4,500 to my name, a few pieces of furniture and nothing else to show for twenty years of marriage. Except of course, my beloved daughter – the light of my life. My love for her carried me when love for myself did not.

LIVING (AND FIGHTING TO LIVE) THE LIFE I WAS MEANT TO LIVE

Every year after the divorce, I still faced battles. Each year I grew stronger. Whenever the failure of Sassytails threatened to defeat me, I reminded myself to keep moving forward one day at a time. Anytime I was tempted to look externally for the answer, I shifted my focus to the power inside and ignited the power within first. I chose to trust the process in hopes that someday it would all make sense. When my inside changed – and I mean truly changed - everything shifted.

The real proof for me today is watching my 20-year-old daughter view the world very differently. While her narrative is still being written, I have seen evidence that she is close friends with the green zone of the sisterhood. Back in 2013, my mental model of the Sassytails experience was a complete failure. I had branded myself with an F on my forehead. Heather taught me to see it differently when she completed an essay on an application for a math and science school when she was fifteen years old. Here are her words -

> *I have been in the business world since I was six, when my mom and I started a company called Sassytails. . . . At eight years old, I spoke to hundreds of high school students about entrepreneurship. I worked with a media team to write a script and star in a* Harry Potter video[1] *for our company.*

---

1   YouTube.com/KimberlyFaithInspires - find video titled "A Look at a Past Chapter - Sassytails"

. . . our story was even featured in the <u>Wall Street Journal</u>[2].

Launching this company, I learned how much work it takes to create something you really want. . . Despite our success, our investor team made some mistakes, which led us to make hard business decisions. These mistakes led to the closing of Sassytails. I was eleven years old.

Through this experience, I learned not only about the business world but also how to fail with grace. (That was the sentence that made me cry!) *Learning about failure at a young age has shaped the person I am today. It has made me not afraid of it. In my opinion, it is a part of life that everyone goes through. . . . I consider myself lucky this whole Sassytails experience has made me not afraid of any challenge.*

Sometimes, it is from our children that we learn the most. My daughter sees the world through a different lens, and for that I am grateful.

My new life today is very different because I am a different person – emotionally, physically, spiritually, and energetically. This new life has taught me that the sisters are like us: multidimensional. When I thought I knew the green zone of Jalila by owning my value at work, she showed me there is an entirely different dimension to owning your value when blending two families together. The learning continues.

When we do the work and go the distance with these mental models, the world comes into focus. When we see the Narrative is playing out, we can say to ourselves, *I don't think so, sister. Not going there today.* And then, driven by the love we have for others, we are *compelled* to spread the message. You want other women to experience the freedom for themselves.

CIRCLE OF LIFE: REWRITING OUR PERSONAL NARRATIVE FIRST

During those difficult years, I was trapped by the red zones of many of the sisters. I remember in vivid detail what it was like. The expectation of perfection was my constant companion. It seemed everywhere I turned, I wasn't enough. I was overwhelmed doing everything I thought I *had* to do. I was constantly seeking approval, only I did not realize that consciously. I apologized for breathing oxygen and even taking up space on the planet. I was convinced that everyone else's opinion was more important than my own. I told myself to accept the status quo. Even when everything inside of me was screaming otherwise. The list goes on and on. What was the collective impact of drowning in the red zone? **I gave away my personal power**. Like Dorothy with ruby slippers walking down the yellow brick road, I had the power all along but I could not see it at the time.

Through my journey with the Sisterhood and learning to shift into the green zone of freedom, I made three life-altering, powerful discoveries. These discoveries resulted in a transformation of my life and my purpose.

1. **Shift to the offensive**. There is a big difference between being on the defensive and being on the offensive. Much like the difference between victimhood and victory. Every decision we make is driven by feeling powerless or

powerful. Each decision is rooted in fear or love. Yet we don't often slow down long enough to ask ourselves the question. Every time I was facing a battle, fear always led me to a defensive position which was a powerless place to be. The only time I was able to gain ground was when I shifted my mindset to the offensive. When I shifted to the energy of love - even if it was simply love for myself. Love propels us forward. When I stepped into powerful mindsets, the fears grew smaller. When I stopped fueling the fear, it lost its luster. Drama, Powerlessness, and Just faded into the background. When I changed internally, everything externally began to change.

2. **Respect is an inside job first.** Once I stopped giving in to fear, I was startled to find the world responded. When I respected myself and owned the power that had been inside all along, everyone – including men – started to treat me differently. The sheer vibration and life force I radiated set in motion a very different reality. I reached a place where I would not, could not, tolerate disrespect on any level. I started to boldly claim my value one small step at a time, and guess what? Others started to respond. That is when the ah-ha became crystal clear. Changing my external world required me to change my internal world first. As within, so without.

That understanding also led to a shift on my perspective of men. Instead of viewing them as the enemy or as ones to be feared – as life and the Narrative had taught me - I learned to embrace the true partnerships we can have together. The offensive mindset I chose for myself changed everything. If I was not respected, then I removed myself from the situation. All of a sudden they realized this was no longer an optional game. It was either give the respect I was due or . . . wait, there was no "or." It was either respect or nothing.

There is a fine line to walk when it comes to stepping into our power *and* working with the other 50% of humanity we know as our sons, husbands, brothers, friends, and colleagues. Results matter to men. It is really much simpler than we realize. We can learn to speak their language- a language rooted in results. They can learn to speak our language as well. They will treat us with respect when we give it to ourselves first - and then demand it - in a calmly confident, calmly passionate manner. The unintended consequence of our tolerating disrespectful behavior for so long is that in effect we have had a hand in training them to not take us seriously. While we are shifting the way we think to stop accepting the unacceptable, it is important we don't allow the pendulum to swing to a male bashing culture. As women, we are designed to birth, to create. And that means creating a culture of love and acceptance. Tough love, yes, but love nevertheless. We don't have to subject ourselves to poor behavior by anyone.

Many are encouraging us to have different[3] conversations[4] about this very issue as we should. Like it or not, men and women are in this boat called life together. It serves no one for one side or the other to be beaten down. This is a critical understanding in the circle of life. Yes, the masculine energy is out of alignment and it is gobbling up humanity. That we can't control. The only way to change the momentum and stop the downward spiral is for the feminine energy to rise up in equal strength. This we *can* control. Day by day, decision by decision.

We all know men and women think very differently. Men often tend to be linear thinkers. If there is problem, solve it. The concern is then checked off the to-do list; onto the next problem. Women can often see beyond the immediate problem/solution dilemma. Most women are naturally wired to look farther down the road and anticipate unintended consequences. This is the reason women can juggle many responsibilities all at once. While men are busy pushing one domino at a time, unaware of the future problems being created as result of that "solution," women have the innate ability to 'see' the entire circle of dominos. While both approaches have pros and cons, women can embrace how powerful this interconnected way of thinking really is. When I truly embraced this realization, it rocked my world. Yes, the hand that rocks the cradle is the hand that rules world; however, rocking the cradle is simply the BEGINNING of our power to transform the world.

3. **Create a life of choice.** When we have choices, we have power. There are a multitude of reasons why many women have not been able to create a life of choice; however, we are entering a spectrum of time where we can change that reality. We are at the precipice of a tipping point for the empowerment of women. Having the freedom to walk away from disrespect speaks volumes. When we stop investing time banging our head against the wall of his-story, we free up the emotional energy to write her-story one page at a time.

This is all possible in your world, too. Yes, there is a razor-thin line between giving in and leaning in. The temptation to give in is not what defines us. The choice we make at that intersection does.

A Message from Kim

YourLionInside.com Video 4

When We Are Tempted to Give In

The loss of Kailyn is a sobering reminder of what can happen when we lose our way. The Narrative can feel like quicksand drawing us in. The more we fight, the deeper we sink. We grow tired of fighting the status quo and wonder if things will ever change. How can we still be fighting issues like sexual harassment in the workplace? Weren't those battles supposed to be won decades ago? Weren't we liberated when the Feminine Mystique started a revolution in 1963? We wonder if our small actions even matter. After all, we are but one person, right? We wonder about the future for our daughters, granddaughters, nieces and the young women we mentor.

The exhaustion is real.

The weariness is tedious.

There are times when giving in, instead of leaning in, seems like the only realistic alternative. When you find yourself at that intersection – wondering if your actions matter - know that they do matter. Take heart in knowing YOU matter.

Earlier in this book, you were introduced to the concept of igniting your power within. Now, armed with the Toolkit and inspired by the Sisterhood, you have the ability to ignite – to tap into - your power within. Seeing through the Narrative and embracing the power of the Sisterhood for our own life first is the key that will unlock the collective shift we desire. When we change our inner dialogue – and what we see in the mirror each day - the collective power to create a world that truly values women will follow. Yes, we stand on each other's shoulders as we build on our success but ultimately, the answer is within. **The answers we seek will never lie outside of us**. Every time we pause, reflect and consciously choose our direction, we create a new reality – individually and collectively.

As women, the power to carry and birth a new life belongs to us alone. However, we have the power to create so much more: a new movement, a new reality for ourselves, a new future for humanity. The power to accomplish all this lies inside each of us. When you fully embrace all the power available to you right now, the effects ripple across the world. Small actions have BIG impact; it's called the butterfly effect, which is the notion that one small action can ripple across the system. If you have ever been heartbroken over stories of child brides, female genital mutilation, the killing of baby girls, the abuse of women or the economic poverty facing women, and you have found yourself feeling powerless, pause long enough to recognize the Narrative for what it is: a lie of epic proportions that has dimmed the light in all of us.

Look in the mirror right now. The reflection you see – your lion inside – has the power to change the world. That is the Truth, and Truth will always change the landscape we know as reality. This is the grand adventure beckoning to us all.

WHAT IS TRULY AT STAKE?

Let us be very aware of what is truly at stake. On February 23, 2017, I was leading a three-day training program for a group of corporate women identified as high-potential leaders for a global company of 180,000 employees. We were in a quaint village a few kilometers outside of Paris, France. For three days, we worked on enhancing their executive presence, building their leadership brand and improving their overall communications skills. As with many sessions like this before, the bulk of the work was in reminding each of them how talented they really were. The Narrative had done quite a job of dimming the light – the power - within. My job was to be a mirror that allowed each of these women to see in themselves what I could so clearly see: talented women with an unbelievable amount of power waiting to be unleashed.

It came to the last day of the program, and Aki, a talented young woman from India, was preparing to present a speech. Throughout our time together, I had noticed an unusual characteristic in Aki: any time she had something to say, she would simply start talking and wouldn't stop until everyone else in the room had no choice but to be quiet. It did not matter who was talking or what the subject was. It was quite disconcerting at times. I was baffled about how to address it. As I was helping Aki get ready to go out on stage and give her presentation, I asked her about this communication technique. In those few moments, I could see and feel the intense fear surrounding that subject for her. She was having difficulty articulating why she communicated in that manner. In that awkward moment of silence, I finally understood what was really happening.

That characteristic – the very one that the rest of us in the session were baffled by – was a sign of strength in the region of India where she was from. It was what she had to do EVERY SINGLE DAY TO EVEN HAVE A CHANCE TO BE HEARD. She literally had to steamroll over the men in her culture simply to get a word in edgewise. It was the only way she ever had a voice. Time did not allow for reflection; it was time for her to present to the class.

Aki walked slowly to the front of the room to begin her presentation. As she started to speak, her voice began to shake and the tears started to fall. She was visibly shaken by our previous conversation. No one spoke a word. My heart was breaking with hers. It was a moment of truth unlike any other I had experienced in my twenty years of training. The class was baffled about what was unfolding. After a moment of heartfelt consideration, I walked onstage, stood next to Aki, and told the class about our previous conversation.

Then the magic happened.

I watched as this group of women from seven different countries came together to support Aki in that moment of uncertainty. Rashida, a brave leader from the U.K., said with absolute conviction, "Aki, we know you don't have this kind of support in your world, but I want you to know you have it right now. And it does not have to stop with this training class. You are one of us, and we are right here to encourage you every step of the way." The powerful commentary continued. For the first time in her life, Aki was experiencing a professional sisterhood. She took a deep breath and composed herself. Emboldened by the strength of the women surrounding and supporting her, Aki delivered her presentation with power. It was an amazing moment that transcended age, race and nationality, defined by the transformational power of sisterhood. It is a sisterhood that truly has the power to change the world, one woman at a time.

On the long flight home, as I was replaying the powerful moments of the program in my mind, it hit me. I now knew what was truly at stake. I finally understood what the Sisterhood had been trying to tell me all along.

If those of us living in countries today that allow us the "freedom" to fully embrace our power don't do it, then our sisters like Aki in other countries don't have a chance.

We are part of a much larger collective story, playing out day after day across the world. I returned home with a renewed passion to inspire every woman to fully embrace the power she does have. I am on a quest to inspire women across the globe to shift their lives from the weakness of the red zone to the power of the green zone. To shift from living life small - like a kitten – to a life fueled by the power of a mighty lion. When we find ourselves tempted to give in instead of lean in, think of Aki and sisters like her around the world. Every single day, we can choose to embrace the power available to us. Because in fact, we are lucky to have it.

A week after the program, I received an email from Rashida, the British woman who had supported Aki so powerfully . . .

"I am traditionally a bit of a cynic when it comes to leadership coaching, but you reset my views . . . you made me realize that us ladies can be who we are: strong, empathetic and supportive for each other without losing respect. A genuine and heartfelt thanks. I don't normally work well with other women, especially when it comes to receiving feedback. You somehow created a constructive, supportive and safe place for us to try out new techniques without fear – and with a group of women who are

usually deeply competitive in the room - it was quite something to see!" R.G. from the U.K.

We truly can shift our focus from fear to faith – in ourselves and in each other – once we understand what is truly at stake.

THE LEVERAGE

The surprising leverage inherent in this entire book is that women are more than willing to go the distance for others. When we can't muster up enough love for ourselves, we tap into the deep reservoir of love we have for others. Fear can be a barrier to us personally; however, courage bubbles up from the depths of our soul when it comes to protecting someone – or something – else. Think mama bear syndrome on steroids. Whether it is the passion we have for our family, our children, our pets or for humanity, this legacy of love is powerful enough to redefine the Narrative as we know it today.

Keep in mind, the Narrative is rooted in a one-sided view of the world. Everything we have been taught is driven by history. When we see "history" for what it really is – *his* story – we finally understand what has been missing. We can see the half-written book we were given at birth for what it really is. Let us close that book and shift our focus to the beautiful, blank pages waiting for us. The time has come to write her-story.

What could the world look like if we paused long enough to see the world through a new lens of "her-story?" How would the world be different? Without the expectations that have been placed on our shoulders, without the judgment that has weighed us down, without the "should" that we have been carrying for a century, what would her-story look like? Is it possible?

It is absolutely possible.

Women are designed to create, and this ability to create is the source of our power.

CORPORATIONS CAN'T DO IT ALONE

Every time we read a workplace report on diversity, we are only "seeing" through one lens. It does not give us a clear picture of reality. The sobering truth is if every diversity and gender equality initiative was 100% successful, we would inevitably run into the reality that our internal dialogue is still standing in the way. Every woman's story in this book, and countless others, are living holograms of this reality. However, once women changed their internal mindset, everything shifted. **It was an inside job first.**

Yes, corporations need to continue probing into the inequities. Yes, we need to continue partnering with men to create new realities for us all. Let us not lose sight of the fact that there are many good men out there fighting for us as well. Having said that, yes, sexual harassment must be rooted out at every level. As I write this final chapter, the #MeToo movement is igniting a new wave of conversation and awareness. Many of the distorted expectations that have been considered normal are beginning to be dismantled, brick by brick; however, our work – individually and collectively – is just beginning. We are at the precipice of a ceiling-shattering window of time, watching as the shift unfolds with momentum many thought they would never see in their lifetime. The heartbreaking USA Gymnastics case of a predatory doctor is yet another example of how the world is significantly changing. Each time justice was driven by a woman who shifted her internal perspective FIRST to ignite a wave of change. We have a front-row seat to what happens when those who have abused their power are held accountable.

This issue of people abusing power is not a new story. It is important to understand a key reason Susan B. Anthony fought so hard for the right to vote. She and her fellow warriors were heartbroken over women who were abused – emotionally and physically. There are many stories of her sheltering women and children who were fleeing domestic violence situations – much of it driven by alcohol abuse. She knew women would remain powerless if they could not influence policy at every level.

Think about the significance of this for a moment. The suffrage movement led by Susan B. Anthony and others was driven by a desire to give women power over their lives and by the belief that the answers to their troubles would come from society and from those in power. The writings of these suffragettes reveal their genuine belief that fighting for the right to vote would solve the issues facing women. They had every reason to think the answer was external. However, if that was true, then why are we living with the following statistics nearly one hundred years later?

- Nearly 1 in 4 women in the U.S. have experienced severe physical violence by an intimate partner in their lifetime.

- More than half of all American women—54%—have experienced "unwanted and inappropriate sexual advances" at some point in their lives according to a recent poll; 33 million U.S. women have been sexually harassed in work-related episodes.

- In the U.S., and abroad, 1 in 4 young people don't think it's serious if a guy who is normally gentle sometimes slaps his girlfriend when he's drunk and they're arguing.

The statistics provide a snapshot of reality. In many cases, the statistics for our sisters globally are even more heartbreaking. Perhaps there is an additional sobering dynamic at play in this larger story. **Is it possible that we have invested so much of our emotional bandwidth into looking outside of ourselves** - for power, for blame, shifting from one defensive move to another - that we have missed opportunities to significantly shift the internal dialogue of which the Sisterhood speaks? Is it possible that once we truly embrace the empowering mindsets each sister has revealed to us, we will shift our internal expectations to such a degree that we will not be able to tolerate the pervasive disrespect that is at the heart of the statistics above? Can you consider the possibility that today, in 2018, we are facing a crossroads of epic proportions - a life-altering intersection - where we have a chance to shift our future by shifting our internal dialogues? I believe it is quite possible.

Apparently, we are still passing on a lot more than basic genetics.

EXAMINING WHAT WE INHERIT AND WHAT WE KEEP

Remember the pot roast parable? Two subsequent generations behaved in a certain way – cutting off the ends of the pot roast - simply following information that was unconsciously passed on. No big discussions. It was not written down as part of the recipe. It simply happened in the busy-ness of life. The action was filed away as part of their "how to make pot roast" mental folder. And those unwritten rules stuck. Were the mother and daughter to blame for following in the grandmother's footsteps? Of course not. But let's dissect what happened as an example of how we come to embrace the "way we do things around here" unconsciously.

The grandmother grew up at a time when retail stores were not abundant – no nearby Costco or Walmart offering the wide array of cookware that we take for granted today. She probably lived in a smaller home, keeping only what was needed. And like all good women impacted by the Depression era, she did her best to be frugal.

Growing up, the mother learned how to cook from the grandmother. They probably spent a lot of time in the kitchen together and doing household chores. The mother was taught all the skills needed to be a "good wife." The mother absorbed the lessons with and without the rules being spoken. All we have to look at is a toddler today mimicking a parent or older sibling and we see it in action. Ever wonder where the old adage "do as I say, not as I do" came from? It would be safe to assume the mother had access to more retail stores than the grandmother did - the world was changing. It was common to have more cookware in the kitchen. Economic prosperity was on the rise. Perhaps her home was larger with a bigger kitchen. It is likely her family was better-off than the generation before.

Now we think of the daughter, the new bride. Her world is dramatically different from the world her grandmother and mother knew. In her mother's day, there was no internet and – gasp – no Amazon! The newlywed likely went to college. By the time she got married, there were bridal showers with gift registers. Far from utilitarian in nature, things for the kitchen were purchased based on how they looked and whether they were from the recent Kate Spade collection. As for cooking, it is likely the newlywed did not spend a lot of time in the kitchen with her mom. Perhaps her mother went back to work once the divorce was final. Perhaps the mother read *The Feminine Mystique*, liberating her from a path she was expected to take. Regardless, the newlywed is now a busy professional along with her new husband. There are so many trendy restaurants to try that the time spent cooking is limited. When they made the pot roast, she was more focused on her adorable new cookware to second-guess cutting the ends off the pot roast. It was automatic, like being on autopilot. After all, they were busy garnishing the pot roast. She wanted to snap a photo and post it on Instagram.

And this brings us right back to where we are today – a world away from a generation ago, right?

In many ways, we have changed women's reality:

- The Feminine Mystique, a bestseller published in 1963, was crucial to explaining "that which has no name" - the prevailing belief that as a woman, fulfillment had only one definition: housewife-mother.

- Women's participation in the U.S. labor force has climbed from 32.7 percent in 1948 to 56.8 percent in 2016.

- The proportion of women with college degrees in the labor force has almost quadrupled since 1970. More than 40 percent of women in the labor force had college degrees in 2016, compared with 11 percent in 1970.

- The range of occupations women workers hold has also expanded, with women making notable gains in professional and managerial positions.

- Efforts to increase women in STEM are actively addressing the issue that only 35% of undergraduate degrees in engineering go to women.

- Storybooks and toys for girls are dismantling stereotypes by expanding to include what was traditionally seen as "boy interests."

All this is good news. But the real question – the elephant in the room –is **why are we tolerating disrespectful behavior** - personally or professionally? The answer: the Narrative has convinced us we have to. We have been listening to the Narrative for so long, we can't even see what her-story might look like. Here is a glimpse into what it could look like to inspire you to think - and see – differently:

- Instead of sexual harassment training that instills fear in the workplace, we invite our daughters to be part of the training. Imagine asking each dad to explain to his daughter face-to-face what kind of treatment she should expect in the workplace. We have the power to shift the conversation from #MeToo to #ourdaughters. Fear is never enough for sustainable change. Love is.

- When we go in to negotiate a salary, we are ALL asking questions about a workplace free from sexual harassment, pay equity and flexibility. If the job requires travel, we ask whether we will be supported to stay in hotels that are safe. We boldly ask for the higher salary – remembering our sisters like Aki – knowing when we negotiate for one, we negotiate for all. Leaving behind a mindset driven by fear, we step into a mindset focused on what we bring to the table.

- We bravely bring to light any behavior that does not respect us, individually or collectively. We create a life of choice that allows us to pursue other options as needed. Results are what matter to those in power. When we stop choosing to allow our blood, sweat and tears to make them more money therefore giving them more power, then things will begin to change. The #MeToo movement is an emboldened example of what can happen when we say "enough!" When frat boy behavior rears its head, we now have the tools to say stop –

> **S**hout
>
> **T**o the world
>
> **O**ur collective
>
> **P**ower to drive change.

- We have conversations with our daughters and the young women we mentor painting a new vision for the future. We make a conscious choice to refuse to keep the Narrative alive by giving its tired old storylines any more power; instead, we focus our energy on writing her-story.

- We boldly step out on behalf of all sisters when it comes to negotiating salaries, hiring suppliers, and any opportunity that arises to ellevate pay equity for all of us. May the story of the joint salary negotiations by Jessica Chastain and Octavia Spencer inspire us to think and behave differently. We are stronger together!

- We encourage our sons, husbands, friends and co-workers – all the men in our world – to understand that to receive the respect they so desperately crave, treating others with respect first is the key. Remember, men have their own Narrative to dismantle. We can draw boundaries with men while still caring for them.

As women, we are designed for tough love and fully equipped to be love warriors for humanity.

We are entering a golden age of transparency and respect. We are entering an era where we can no longer live a divided life - where we are one person in front of the world and another behind closed doors. The universe is calling us to bring to light that which has been standing in the shadows. The good news is there is freedom on the other side of a divided life. Despite how it might appear at first glance, this is an exciting time for humanity. It is a time that offers each of us an open invitation to write her-story. Literally, and figuratively, humanity depends on it.

INFLUENCING THE DNA OF THOUGHT

The Sisterhood reminds us that the pervasive powerlessness holding us back is anchored by one thing: **what we believe about ourselves.**

It is the subtle nuances that are still tucked away in the DNA of our thoughts that are impacting us now. We are on autopilot, blinded to our own power to change how we see the world. The limiting thoughts show up in unexpected, unconscious and silent ways. This book is my attempt to map out the misfiring in the DNA sequence still impacting women today. It is a divine vehicle sending a message that you – yes YOU - have the power to create a different world. You are an atom of change. It is within our grasp to shift the DNA of thought so it will positively influence generations to come. Consciously choose to unplug from the Narrative. Shift your focus from what everyone has told you your world has to be to what it *could* be. Redefine it on your own terms. Shift from breaking the rules to *making* the rules. The significance of your life and your personal power is transformational – individually and collectively. The world is ripe for this alchemy of thought.

The generations before us had little choice but to see the world through his-story; however, we live in an unprecedented time where we don't have to. Remember the teenager vs. toddler example - where the system grew up but the mindsets did not? It is time for our mindsets to consciously catch up. We are facing a crossroads - a critical intersection – collectively and individually. We can choose to set his-story aside and ask ourselves each day with each choice "what could **her**-story look like?"

We each play a key role in dismantling the internal dialogues tap dancing subconsciously in our minds. Remember the balanced lens through which to see the world? Both are desperately needed. It is my deep desire that we will not need to have these same conversations one hundred years from now. And that means we need to embrace new ways of thinking today.

The only way we will create a culture that truly values women is to embrace collective change and individual change with equal intensity. But know that individual change always comes first. Individual change is the catalyst. I learned this first hand – and so can you.

CHANGE IS A CONTINUUM

In today's world, so many want a formula, a template, five easy steps to the end goal. However, the journey to finding your lion inside is very different for each of us. It's a journey that involves change, and there's no formula for that. Change is a continuum that allows space for a new reality to be revealed.

We can't control the changes, but we can empty the toxicity in our life and make room for the new and good. We can't see her-story when we are so busy fighting his-story. We cannot shift to an offensive position in life as long as we are on the defensive. A new reality cannot emerge when our current reality is overflowing with judgment – from ourselves or from others.

TEN YEARS AGO

Ten years ago, I was in survival mode, drowning in the red zone. This is what my lion inside meant to me then -

Limit the damage others can do to me

Independence – find it!

Own my yes

Now is the only time that matters

FIVE YEARS AGO

I was newly divorced and learning to simplify life. I was starting to unplug from the Narrative. I made conscious choices to detach from the drama. I started to move into the yellow zone of many of the sisters.

Live

Inspired.

Own my

New story.

NOW IN 2018

I have been living in the green zone of freedom for years now. I now see the Narrative very clearly. I powerfully choose a new reality for myself every day.

Love and laugh often

Inspiration is my essence

Open my eyes to her-story

New narrative – create it for myself and for my sisters around the world

What story is your lion inside inviting you to write today? Dare to listen. Your heart knows.

L _____

I _____

O _____

N _____

"Tap into the power within," the Sisterhood beckons. "Your lion inside is waiting to lead you towards a new reality – for you and for your sisters around the globe. Day by day, decision by decision."

WE ARE THE HERO WE SEEK

You may wonder if the sisters will ever go away. Will there be a time when a mindset holding us back will be gone for good?

Some sisters go away once we have learned all we need from them. Like loved ones we have lost, we hold onto the lessons they shared with us, keeping the gift they gave us close to heart. And we remain grateful they were a part of our lives.

Other sisters will be with us for a lifetime – and we become better at bringing out their best. When a challenging situation arises, threatening to bring back the old mindsets, we cycle through it faster. Today, in the company of the Sisterhood, what took two years to process before now only takes two weeks. You'll be able to quickly recognize the mindsets that no longer serve you much faster, and you will *consciously* choose a different mindset. Therein lies the power of the Sisterhood, for the rest of your life.

I am now thankful for the Sassytails experience. It was the leverage for my life. It taught me who I was when everything I knew was stripped from me. Everything was brought into question. My ability to trust my judgment about others and myself was shattered. Faith in my future was nonexistent. I set out to discover who I was without of the trappings I had called "my life." Who I was without money, without a title. Who I was with no story.

When it comes to failure, there is such a thing as hitting rock bottom. When you cannot disappoint people any more than you've already disappointed. When you cannot shatter expectations any more than they are already shattered. A place where there is truly nowhere to go but up – and surprisingly, that's a freeing realization. No matter what, the sun comes up every day. As we learn to embrace Kari's message of *I am enough*, we find great strength. That strength gives us the courage to be vulnerable and to share our stories . . . failures and all. There is great value in those experiences in spite of – and sometimes because of – their not-so-great ending. People need to know there is life beyond failure, whether it is personal or professional. We must help each other remember that as long as we have the ability to love, we can make a difference in this world. The rest can be overcome with time.

We build these stories into our lives and we live them out. *Things are okay,* we tell ourselves, *as long as we live out the script.* But when the story is shattered - the pages ripped out of the storybook, leaving us with nothing but a tattered cover - we ask in bewilderment, *what now*? To my sisters who have been there, you know of what I speak.

You set out on a journey to figure out what matters. It took a while to accept the notion that as long as I could give another human being a hug, life was worth living. If I could offer <u>one</u> word of encouragement to another, that was enough. Without money. Without the trappings of success we are taught is the goal. Without prestige, power or fame, I was enough. I could still be a wonderful mother. I could still break the generational bondage that had tied my family in knots. I could still birth new ideas – one of which you are holding in your hands right now.

It was not until many, many years later I understood some of the distorted thinking that impacted the Sassytails chapter of my life. It started with good intentions - as so many things in life do. Now that I understand energy and intention, I see it more clearly. The intention behind Sassytails was *desperation*. I was trying to prove myself to the world. I was fighting everyone and everything. The good I was hoping to spread was overshadowed by the fear I had inside. The change I was trying to make was overshadowed by my inability to trust my own decisions. The genuine love I had for inspiring young girls was overshadowed by the lack of love I had for myself. In a nutshell, I was trying to break free from the Narrative – the 21st century variation of what *The Feminine Mystique* labeled " that which has no name" decades ago.

This path led me to the place where I finally love myself enough. As much as I love my daughter. It is a wonderful place to be.

My life path gave me an opportunity to unplug from the Narrative. Although I didn't know it at the time, when I started investing energy into creating my story, I set aside much of what I was taught from his-story. I started from a blank page, which became an important page in *her-story*. Ten years later, here I am.

The defining difference in the gift you now hold in your hands vs. the experience of Sassytails? Everything has shifted. I have the same desire to make a difference, but this time, the intention flows from <u>love</u>. Love for myself, love for others, love for my daughter. Love for my sisters around the globe and a heartfelt devotion that transcends time, space and differences.

This time I have nothing to prove. I am enough, and I know that with every cell in my body. The Sassytails experience obliterated everything I once believed.

And *that* has made all the difference.

THE POWERFUL LIFE WAITING FOR YOU

When you print the one-page inspiration at YourLionInside.com of the Sisterhood, make a conscious choice to shift your focus to the green zone. *What we focus on grows.* If you are tempted to focus on the red zone and stop doing these things, then the journey will feel hard. It does not have to be hard. Any time you feel powerless, use the guide to find your way. The green zone is where the power is. Focus on these empowering mindsets and the rest will fall away. The Sisterhood has given us a treasure map to freedom.

What does that freedom look like? I was hoping you would ask . . .

Conclusion

"Intention supported by repetition
eventually creates your truth."

Jabine - My Guardian Angel

THE ART OF TRANSFORMATION

"I think we should tell them," Darsha says to the Sisterhood.

"It was an important lesson for me too," Avalene agrees. "Share it with them, Kari."

"As you live your life consciously with the Sisterhood, remember there are only two choices: victimhood or victory," Kari says. "Yes, there may be shades in between as you learn," she pauses. "However, at the end of the journey, your life will be evidence of which side of the Sisterhood you danced with. There is always a choice."

"I like to think of it like music," Nikki adds.

"Music?" Gabi asks.

"Yeah. Our thoughts are like music. We can tune into our thoughts like we tune into our favorite kind of music. You know, like a streaming app or radio station," says Nikki.

"I see what you mean. Tune into the station for the type of music you *want* to hear," Ranee says. "Change *the station on your self-talk radio,* sisters!"

The Sisterhood laughed.

"Change your words, change your world," Kari says. "Words create thoughts. Thoughts are the codes that unlock your creation of this thing called your *life*."

"Do you think they will do it, Kari?" asks Avalene. "Will they will change their station?"

Nikki speaks up instead. "I have hope they will choose to harness our power everyday."

The Sisterhood smiles in agreement.

What would life be like if we consciously chose to live by these seven empowering mindsets? Say them out loud to yourself right now. Repeat three times slowly . . .

> I am enough
> Here is what I am willing to do
> I can move forward in confidence
> I choose to rewrite the narrative
> There is enough for me & you
> I own & articulate my value
> My power is much needed in this world

Truth and Simplicity have been trying to tell us that deep down, *we already are all these things*. Everything else is the <u>illusion</u>. Everything else is the dust that has dimmed the beauty of the jewels we are.

Everything else has blinded us to the power within. Everything else – the noise, the judgment, the drama - is causing us to meow like a kitten when we have the strength to roar like a lion.

THIS IS THE LIFE WAITING FOR YOU . . .

When you embrace the truth that I am enough . . .

You'll realize you no longer have to strive. You no longer have to buy into the mythical mindset that *I have to do more, be more, give more.* You'll realize you don't have to be anything except who you are. Great freedom and peace comes with this realization. You will find a lifetime of wisdom in three small words: ***I am enough.***

When you live from the mindset of here is what I am willing to do.

When you choose to jump into the driver's seat of life, you won't be taking Victimhood or Just along with you for the ride. You'll compassionately understand many are still blinded by the old mindsets, but you are free. When the world tries to entice you back into the old ways, you'll smile knowingly and hold your ground. And when the chatter begins to overwhelm, you'll know it's time to find a quiet place to recharge and refocus, if only for a moment.

You'll calmly draw boundaries knowing that when you love yourself enough, you will then be able to love and lead others well. You cannot love from a depleted heart. You cannot grow a fertile life if your reservoir is dry. If being selfish is thinking only of yourself and being selfless is thinking only about others, you choose to be *self-full.* And you are the only one who can make that decision. You are responsible for your own life.

When you move forward in confidence.

Living *with* confidence means you're taking something with you – adding more weight to your backpack of life. Living *in* confidence means there's an essence within you that radiates from the inside out. And such *confidence inside* allows you to:

- Recognize that some people still believe the old mindsets that you, too, once believed.

- Realize that it will take time for others to understand and accept your new perspective.

- Take responsibility for how you might have unknowingly trained others to treat you.

- No longer wait for others to accept you or give you permission to live the life you are meant to live.

- Make your own choices with understanding, conviction, and compassion – knowing that when you make a choice to better your life, it will ultimately better the lives of others.

- Tolerate the tension between where you are today and where you want to be.

- Refuse to hang out with Guilt, Blame or any of the mean girls of your mindset. You sent those girls packing a long time ago.

Recognize when the Narrative is trying to put you in your place and refuse to buy into the prevailing worldview.

When you no longer have to consciously "rewrite the Narrative"

It is now woven into the DNA of your thoughts. You've stepped out of the cage you placed yourself in and now the world is full of possibilities. Whenever the red zone of one of the sisters surprisingly shows up or the world throws a curve-ball, you respond and rebound quickly because a long time ago, you made the choice to befriend Victory over Victimhood. **When you truly believe "there is enough for me and you."**

You take pride in believing you are the right one for the opportunity. You take more risks. You go after stretch assignments. That job you once thought was out of reach? Now you apply for it. Or you run for the elected position. Understanding there's always risk when you reach, you still go after new opportunities and if things don't turn out as hoped, you can accept it. You don't label yourself a failure; instead, you think "not this time." You accept things happen for a reason and do an honest assessment of growth opportunities. If you know deep down you did your best, then you rest in the knowing there is another path. If truthful consideration reveals you did not, you then commit to do the work to move in that direction.

You no longer have to tear others down – men or women - because you know they can succeed AND you can succeed. We all have different gifts to bring to the world. You choose to be ready for the next assignment, the next opportunity, or the next challenge that calls for what only you have to offer. You don't waste precious time allowing Judgement to do her thing. Instead, you invest your energy into building others up. You choose to _detach from the drama_ to which the world is addicted. **When you "own and articulate your value" internally and externally.**

When this happens, it radiates like a light shining from the inside out. You no longer apologize for standing up for yourself, knowing that if you do, it's a disservice to humanity and your sisters. You stand in your truth - *calmly confident, calmly passionate.* When anyone tries to diminish your influence, you now see the Narrative for what it is – and no longer buy into it.

Places or people that cannot or do not appreciate you are slowly carved out of your life. You no longer relate to Victimhood and sent Powerless on her way too. If others don't embrace your personal power, they miss out; but you spend less emotional bandwidth reflecting on it now. You're busy moving forward with a re-energized life, taking delight in new opportunities. You are busy creating a life of choice.

When you fully embrace "your power is much needed in the world."

The time and energy that was once spent tearing others – or yourself – down is now invested in moving forward. You re-alize the ROI of time, energy and emotions is best spent using your power for good, not for harm. Understanding that you have limited emotional bandwidth, you choose wisely – and release the mindsets that no longer serve you or your sisters. The story is no longer only about you; your sisters are always in the back of your mind.

You no longer depend on approval from others to deter-mine your self-worth or listen to those who try to tear you down. They are living in their own powerless world of victim-hood; you see this clearly now. There is no going back. Instead of striving and proving, you walk away *calmly confident, calmly passionate.* You use the love you have for others to pro-pel you forward, knowing it will fuel a love of self.

You find your dharma. You learn why you are here. You invest that time and energy into making a difference. Your focus has shifted: the strength you now have radiates from the inside out and people cannot help but notice and follow.

You tap into that power within, freeing the strength of the lion. When *this* is the life you are living from the inside out, everything shifts. For you. For me. Individually and collectively. Deep down, you know the Truth.

"*It has been there all along,*" the Sisterhood whispers. "*It is done. It is done. It is done.*"

#LegacyofLove

A Message From Kim

YourLionInside.com Video 5

Want to be part of the journey to spread the powerful messages within this book? Go to YourLionInside.com to learn more about hosting a book club.

A Message to My Sweet Sisters

Inspired by our sister Aki and a deep understanding of what is truly at stake, I wrote this on the plane as I traveled home from that program.

To my sisters in Asia – You are a treasure to behold. Wise. Breathtaking in your purity of soul and purpose. It is my heartfelt wish the veil of illusion will fall away. Claim the powerful gifts you have been given for all the world to see.

To my sisters in India – Your strength is deep and wide, yet even you may not see the important role you play in this narrative called *being a woman*. Thank you for your steadfastness. Rest in knowing your steps to break down barriers and forge new paths is not futile. Quite the opposite in fact. And the results are powerful – like a mountain. We can't always see the growth with eyes wide open, yet one day it will appear. Majestic. Tall. Proud.

To my sisters in the U.K. – Such a breath of fresh air you are! News always sounds better when it comes from you. Nothing like a bloody mess to get things moving, right? Keep your energy, spread it far and wide. Many are in need of a dose of your spirit and feistiness.

To my sisters in Europe – Your ability to move among so many cultures is something we can all learn from. There is no one way to define you but you don't mind; you prefer it that way. Your global perspective gives you a unique lens through which to see the world. You inspire us to see life as a kaleidoscope - embracing our differences, admiring the beauty and creating a tapestry of talent.

To my Latina sisters – Your zest for life brings strength to a world in desperate need of kindness. Your ability to love from a full heart is powerful. Your perseverance is unwavering. Your dedication is compelling. May we drink in the magic that is *you*, inspiring us to change the drumbeat of the world one human being at a time.

To my sisters in the Middle East – So many degrees of dizzying expectations threatening to hide the light within. You walk the line, acknowledging all that is steeped in tradition while trying to figure out your heart's calling. Glorious strength. Steadfast courage. Know that we see the treasure you are.

To my sisters in America – You inspire the world with your unwavering dedication, your fearlessness and your sense of individualism. Many march feeling like we have miles to go when it comes to equality. It was truly a revelation when I realized that in the U.S., we are running a sprint compared to our sisters in other countries. They have run three marathons to get to where we stand today. May we all go the distance.

To my sisters I have not yet met – Our paths are destined to cross, somehow, someday, and I can't wait for that day to arrive. Know your spirit has been in my heart as the words have poured onto these pages.

The truth is we are all sisters. When you look past the language barriers, past the traditions, past age differences, past the color of our skin, past the religious beliefs, past the cultural differences, past the expectations placed upon our shoulders, we are all the same. Jewels of all colors, shapes and sizes. Each serving a purpose tied to the collective whole. Each one designed to brilliantly shine.

One last thought, my sisters. Do not be surprised by the pushback you receive – individually and collectively. As we each chip away at the Narrative and as it grows smaller, fear will grow. This is a temporary reaction. Our collective empowerment will render some institutions and systems irrelevant. They will fight to stay alive. Stay the course and draw close to the Sisterhood for strength. It is all part of the

Dance of Change.

A Fabulous Fable for Our Girls

FOR AS LONG AS THERE IS H.O.P.E.

Because it is never too early to start the conversation.

The fella recruited Mable, a spunky little thing with hair that was spiked and eyes that would gleam.

Life had been tough, the fella remembered her sayin.'

May this work give me hope, is what she was prayin.'

So, she set off to task bringing all that she had; a twist and a turn, and gone was the sad. This went on for years, fulfilling and bold; then the undercurrent began, the once warm light running cold.

Little did Mable know, there was a hag in the cella', who prodded and poked the mindset of the fella. The hag once had long curls and lips that twitched; now there was grey and a grimace, and hands holding hips.

The power the hag sought was from others, you see: their talent, their words and even their chi. The hag had not yet discovered her source was inside, from the light we are all born with, meant to keep hope alive.

The hag was lost, focused on envy and greed. Hustling the fella, filling only her needs.

A new castle, fancy shoes, and more filler, the hag said. *Mable's taking what's ours,* she poured into his head; the fella

211

was transfixed, spellbound, sometimes torn; losing sight of what was important, slowly he was worn.

Mable did this, she did that! the fella exclaimed, taking Mable to task, defacing her name. The old hag worked the fella, like a puppet on a string; and blinded by the obvious, he could not see a thing.

Bewildered, Mable asked, *what do I, why does he?* And the chips began to fall, what will be, will be. Mable made a decision: let them reap what they had sewn; it took guts, it took courage, for her to leave what was familiar and known.

For as long as there was H.O.P.E., there was always a chance - to rewrite a new chapter, to take a new stance. Her brain paralyzed by fear, her heart yearning for peace; Mable moved on with her rewrite. Will wonders ever cease?

Mable held her head high and voiced to all; *I am not a victim, I will not take this fall.*

It was in that space, that zone, that clearing of thought; Mable found the peace she so desperately sought. From powerlessness, defeat, fear and trepidation, Mable dug down deep and <u>changed her station.</u>

She said to herself, she said to all – *I choose to own it, I choose to stand tall. I believe in the treasure I was created to be; there is much work to be done for me to be me. I will let my heart shine from here to there.*

Some may not like it, but Mable no longer cared.

SIGH (silence).

The freedom, the peace, did I really win?

Yes, the voice said. *You changed your lens.*

With each step she took, Mable grew stronger and stronger; the smallness of the past was hers no longer.

What started as a meow, ended in a roar; the fear, the defeat, allowed here no more. Awakened at last to the power of her voice, being courageous and brave was Mable's personal choice.

With peace, love, faith, and H.O.P.E., Mable spread this wisdom to all she could find; you too can tap into the power within, for today is but a chance to change your mind.

THE END

Or is it?

Endings and beginnings can be one and the same, blurred by perspective, one of life's little games. When one door closes, another opens wide; trust the path you can't see, and someday you'll know why.

The fella and the hag? Well as you might guess, they are still locked in cages; it's quite a mess. Blinded by ego and poisoned by greed, "we do what we have to" they continue to believe.

While this made Mable sad, she trusted there was a reason. For another, **not her**, would take on that season.

And it was this she said once, twice and more: I AM MABLE, no less, no more. To all from the past and those up ahead, here is one final thought as you settle in bed.

For as long as there is H.O.P.E., there is always a chance to rewrite a new chapter, to take a new stance.

Dedicated to the casualties of egos run amuck —
a celebration of beautiful unintended consequences.

A Message From Kim

YourLionInside.com Video 6

Ways to Spot (and Rewrite) the Narrative

The Narrative shows up around the world on a daily basis, so it's important to be aware of *how* it shows up. In this chapter, you will find examples of how the Narrative can show up and ways it was (or could be) rewritten.

Remember our three-step process:

PAUSE

This step allows you to slow down long enough to recognize *how* the Narrative is showing up. Sometimes, it is hard to see at first glance. Trust your gut. Deep down, you know when something does not feel right. For too long we have been turning off our intuition, but now is the time to turn it **up**, not off. A key indicator is the word <u>should</u>. Sisters, the word *should* is our equivalent to the F-bomb. It is a red flag reminding us that buried deep inside, the Narrative is at play. ***Never bleach a red flag.***

REFLECT

After you pause, consciously choose to **reflect.** Ask yourself, what feels off about this statement or situation? Are you on autopilot, reading a page from his-story, or are you creating her-story from a blank page? Is this action rooted in power or powerlessness? Are you sending a message of victory or victimhood? Is it rooted in love or fear? Are you in a defensive or offensive position? Is there a shift needed that could change the momentum of this event or conversation? Repeatedly asking why (up to seven times) will help you discover what is at the root of the problem. And then, the answers to your questions will clue you in to where you are and open up doors to a new reality – individually and collectively.

CHOOSE

The most powerful step is to **choose.** Shift out of autopilot and *choose* your direction. Consciously *choose* your new path at the intersection. Too many times in life we blow past the intersection without giving it a second thought. Use powerful language: *I can, I will, I am, I choose.*

Journalist Megyn Kelly, one of TIME's Silence Breakers, finds herself at the intersection. "I always thought things could maybe change for my daughter. I never thoughts things could change for me. Never. I believed the system was stacked against women, and the smart ones would understand how to navigate it," she says. "I'm starting to see it so differently now. What if we did complain? What if we didn't whine, but we spoke our truth in our strongest voices and insisted that those around us did better? What if that worked to change reality right now?" May we all remember our power lies in claiming - *I am* powerful. *I can* change the world. *I choose* a new reality for my daughter AND for myself today.

See you at the intersections.

SCENARIO #1: TO UNAPOLOGETICALLY BE MYSELF: WISDOM FROM A LATINA SISTER

"I would definitely say that the intersection of race and gender have informed all of my professional life – I don't shy away from it; I lead with it."

Susana[1] is a corporate communications and public relations professional with 30 years of diverse industry experience. At United Airlines, Susana served as lead external communicator for United's Crisis Center team, implementing all global communications for a 14-day period following the 9/11 attacks. She also worked side-by-side with reporters from *The Wall Street Journal* and *USA Today* on a series of award-winning 9/11 features. With ComEd, she worked on issues of deregulation and reliability as well as several award-winning corporate citizenship programs– including the launch of a $4M new STEM high school in Chicago's West Lawndale community and a Stay-in-School program that earned a White House award for leading efforts in Corporate Citizenship.

Susana agreed to be interviewed because she 100% believes in the premise of this book. She knows first-hand what is was like to change her internal dialogue. She realized the glass ceiling *was* in fact a mirror too.

Here's her story, in her words.

PAUSE – HOW THE NARRATIVE SHOWED UP

"I am a first-generation immigrant, a political refugee from Cuba. I arrived in the United States in the 1960s, when I was two years old. I grew up with three pillars - or challenges - to overcome: gender, ethnicity, and poverty. I was the first person in my family to go to college. Throughout life, I was taught to walk in two worlds: in my authentic, ethnic world and in the white, male world. It was very painful to constantly shut the valve on and off. I found I was never really flowing. I lived with that belief until my mid-30s when I read something that changed my perspective."

REFLECT – A CONVERSATION WITH HERSELF

"I read an article about Mellody Hobson[2], a powerful leader in Chicago. I can still remember what she said about being unapologetically black and unapologetically a woman. Those words changed my world. It was eye-opening to realize I *could* live my life differently. Honestly, that had never occurred to me before. I had listened to everyone else for so long. People of color, and even my bosses, would coach me to live in two worlds. I reached a crossroads – an intersection - and I had a decision to make."

CHOOSE –

WHAT SUSANA CHOSE TO DO AT THE INTERSECTION

"After reading those words, I made a conscious decision to see the world very differently. I chose to start standing in my world and draw others into it. I decided to no longer turn the valve on and off. I started to live authentically and began to gravitate towards jobs where I could live my values. When looking for a new position, I would interview the company as much as they interviewed me. The power shifted. It was an internal shift *first* that changed everything.

"When I lived from that space, my salary ended up matching my value – the value I placed on myself first. This world is in desperate need of people willing to *be themselves* in the corporate world. I now teach young women that you will never

---

2   https://www.vanityfair.com/news/2015/03/mellody-hobson-ariel-investments-fighting-stereotype

find your power as long as you are play-acting. You will never live an authentic life if you are only doing what everyone else has told you to do. If young women can grow up understanding this drumbeat in their heads – that they *can* be themselves – then they can create an entirely different future."

Key Message: Don't shy away from your differences; lead with them.

SCENARIO #2 – THE MYTH OF AGE-ISM

PAUSE – HOW THE NARRATIVE SHOWED UP

Vivian is a vibrant, energetic and talented 52-year-old woman facing a new chapter in life. Her divorce is imminent and she is pursuing new professional opportunities. As she searched for options, she met with several power players in the community - men who have been very successful. She asked for their insight into new opportunities for her. After a few meetings, she called me to share the conversation below.

"He told me I am obviously great at what I do, so I should stick with that instead of trying to reinvent myself for a different career at my age. (I didn't realize hitting 50 was the end of my professional life!) He then told me I should hurry up because no one would hire a 60-year-old speaker, or better yet a 55-year-old speaker! He said right now, I have the advantage of people wanting to stare at me because of my natural beauty."

I could hear the defeat in her voice as she expressed her shock at the conversation. She did not realize she was at an intersection where she could make a choice: buy into his-story OR write her-story instead.

REFLECT – A CONVERSATION BETWEEN SISTERS

"Vivian, I hear the defeat in your voice," I said. *"I know you are trying to hide it. Do you realize that what he said is a myth – a big lie?"*

"I am trying to Kim, but this is a theme in many of my recent meetings," Vivian said. *"Am I really too old now? Am I just fooling myself, thinking I can create a new life at my age?"*

Shift #1 – *"NO, you are not fooling yourself!"* I said. *"Vivian, you have come face to face with the Narrative. This is a tired old storyline that men believe for us, not themselves. Perhaps many grow tired of women as we grow older because we finally wise up and stop tolerating disrespect. This is their story, not your story."*

Shift #2 – *"Why do you keeping looking outside yourself – to these men - for **your** answers?"* I continued. *"They are not going to give you the answers you need to create this new chapter of your life. Can you consider the possibility that you are searching for an answer – a hero – outside yourself?"* Vivian listened intently and recognized it for what it is. *"What do I do with the fear? I am scared about this next phase in my life?"*

Shift #3 – *"Vivian, you have the ability to grow your speaking and consulting business or start a new venture. All the answers you need are inside,"* I said. Vivian replied, *"I guess this is why so many women just go away at this stage of life. . ."* I reminded her that she had the power to change that storyline, starting now.

CHOOSE –

WHAT VIVIAN CHOSE TO DO AT THE INTERSECTION

Vivian made a decision to stop looking outside of herself for the answers. And when the time came to tap into her network of female friends, she remembered that not all women are ready to help other women - yet. Instead of being discouraged by this, she chose to listen to her gut and pay attention. "The women who do want to help show their hearts and intent by actions, not words," Vivian said. Right now, she is happily writing a new business plan – and rewriting the Narrative in the process. Click here to learn more about how to Age Boldly.

Key Message: Slay the dragon of disrespect every time it rears its head.

SCENARIO #3: OPENING COMMENTS FOR A CONFERENCE

PAUSE – HOW THE NARRATIVE SHOWED UP

Sara[3], a high-potential leader in the healthcare field, reached out to me as I was working on this book. She was planning to kick off a women's conference in New York City the following week and wanted my input on her remarks. In light of the Narrative, three opportunities showed up.

REFLECT – A CONVERSATION BETWEEN SISTERS

Shift #1 – For her introductory speech, Sara said she wanted to be brief, to be bright and to be gone. After all, the audience was coming to hear the keynote speakers, not her. *"Whoa,"* I said. I pointed out how this was Nikki's red zone showing up, which says, "I'm okay in the background." *"It is perfectly okay for you to take three minutes to build your leadership brand. No one else is going to do that except you."* Then I learned Sara was the one who helped mobilize the entire event! And she wanted to take a back seat? No way, not happening on my watch.

Shift #2 – As we continued the conversation, Sara commented that the conference was not about her but about the women in attendance. (This is Nikki's red zone sneaking in again.) She wanted to serve them. While her intention was well meaning, it was misdirected. *"One of the best ways you can serve them is to be the best version of yourself, Sara,"* I said. *"There is not a limit to how much shine each of us can have. When you shine, you give others permission to shine."*

Shift #3 – In her opening remarks, Sara planned to share a story, one she had been telling for years, about a struggling artist and how it related to female CEOs and how few there are. *"Sara, you don't seem convinced about this story. Why are you sharing it?"* I asked. She shrugged, *"I don't know. It seems to be the right thing to say. I have never really liked it, but I don't know what else to say."* This was a glaring example of how the Narrative shows up. Sara was inclined to share it because it was the same story *she* had been told over and over again. She was swimming in the fish bowl with the Narrative, and she didn't even know it. Once I pointed it out, she immediately understood. But then the challenge became, what now? Without the old narrative to tell her what to say, she was momentarily speechless.

The conference theme was "Send the Elevator Back Down." I asked what that meant to her. Her immediate response: *be brave.* (She even had the saying written on a Post-it note by her desk.) Still, she was baffled about how to tie it in. She casually mentioned a story about teaching her young daughter to be brave. *Ah-ha!* There was the gold we were seeking -an authentic way to share what deeply mattered to Sara.

CHOOSE –

WHAT SARA CHOSE TO DO AT THE INTERSECTION

She wove together a NEW narrative for her opening remarks, one that was much more empowering. Take a look . . .

I have a note posted in front of my desk to remind me of an important decision I made as I have evolved on my journey as a leader. It says, "Be brave." Two words = BIG impact. Let me explain.

I have a three-year-old daughter named Brooklyn. A few months ago, Brooklyn started gymnastics. I went to drop her off, and I watched kid after kid run in, excited. Brooklyn stood next to me, pulling on my dress, refusing to take one more step. I leaned over and whispered, "Be brave. Being brave means that even though you are scared, you push through and then good things happen." Brooklyn smiled, took a breath and ran off to class. But she left me thinking: Was I being brave in my classroom of life?

I thought about the times in my career when I <u>wasn't</u> brave. When I didn't volunteer for an assignment because I didn't have all the qualifications or when I had a creative idea but just didn't share it. I decided that if I wanted to inspire my daughter to continue being brave, I would have to keep being brave too. Maybe you can relate?

Living up to this idea of "being brave" has encouraged me to say yes when I wanted to say no. To raise my hand to take on one more assignment. I treat each day as an opportunity to be brave. And guess what? Good things happen.

Our event today is due to women making a conscious decision to be brave. A passionate group of

women came together to create a commercial wom-
en's organization. It meant going to our CEO for
support and prioritizing leadership development
for women - among so many competing priorities.
It meant securing funding and being brave enough
to admit that we all needed the inspiration an event
like this provides, no matter where we are on our
leadership journey.

Our theme today is "Send the Elevator Back Down."
And for this to work, we each need to embrace the
idea of being brave - brave enough to step on when
the elevator comes down. In preparing for this event,
I was reminded by another brave woman that the
glass ceiling is often a mirror. And it begs the ques-
tion, do we ever hold ourselves back by not choosing
to be brave?

Ten-minute conversation. Eye-opening shift in perspective. A
world of difference.

Key Message: Be brave and good things will happen.

SCENARIO #4 –WISDOM FROM A SISTER IN THE LARGEST FRATERNITY IN THE WORLD

Kathy[4] is a retired U.S. Army Colonel and has served in a variety of complex roles, including FEMA disaster response, National Defense University Strategic Leadership Program Director, the U.S. Embassy Pakistan, the Pentagon and the White House.

Here, she shares a pivotal moment from a career spent in the largest fraternity in the world: the U.S. military.

PAUSE – HOW THE NARRATIVE SHOWED UP

"I entered the military shortly after Congress mandated that women were allowed in my field. In essence, I was forced upon them. I quickly shifted to survival mode by turning into an android. I stripped away every piece of my femininity so I would not look like a girl. It is amazing how nondescript someone can become when focused on their product, not their person. I became the perfect soldier. That worked until my thirteenth year when a conversation with a mentor changed my perspective."

REFLECT – A CONVERSATION WITH A MENTOR

"Everything you do is perfect," he said. *"You are a perfectionist. You are everything to everyone, but I still don't know who you are. You are a machine. You don't smile. You don't laugh."* After some thought, I responded. *"I have a wall around that piece of myself, sir, and I would rather not share it."* Fortunately, he would not let it go. Over time, he showed me that I could shift to be *who I chose to be instead of who I was molded to be.* He taught me how to put in a sliding glass door to myself so that when I chose to open it, I could. He led

me on a journey of self-awareness and self-examination. Until that point, I lived the military expectations demanded of me - no questions asked."

CHOOSE –

WHAT KATHY CHOSE TO DO AT THE INTERSECTION

"That intersection in life taught me to believe in myself instead of believing in the work I did. My mentor taught me to trust others and to trust myself. I learned power comes with letting go of control; it was an eye-opening lesson. I went on to serve another sixteen years for a total of twenty-nine years and six months. We have to stop saying it's *them*. It has to be *me* owning how I am heard."

AFTER THE INTERSECTION: INSIGHTS
AND ADVICE FROM KATHY

- Truly own your accomplishments and what only you can bring to the situation. Understand and believe that it's not just hard work in the system that brings success rather it's you that brings the magic that makes it all work so well. Contribute from a place of grounded awareness.

- Approach every situation with curiosity and a need to understand the perspectives of others. This will broaden your awareness on issues you think you already understand and open creative new ways to solve problems. Asking instead of telling provides opportunities to synthesize information, changes the breadth and depth of conversations you have with others, and build relationships.

- Relationships don't automatically happen at the group level; they start one on one. Take time to understand what motivates the people around you, and you can begin to develop trusting relationships, one person at a time. These relationships will provide new spaces for people to see and hear you, where actions and words are in alignment with your authentic self.

Key Message: Own how I am heard.

SCENARIO #5 –FOR OUR SISTERS IN HOLLYWOOD AND ENTERTAINMENT

Story based on a viral video of Reese Witherspoon

PAUSE – HOW THE NARRATIVE SHOWS UP

A video of Reese Witherspoon's spirited speech at the 2015 Glamour Women of the Year awards resurfaced in the fall of 2017. For days, my inbox was flooded with emails from those who had seen both the video and read the early versions of this book. *"Look, she saw the Narrative too!"* they told me.

Here's the video; note the phrase that was a glaring example of the Narrative at work. https://www.facebook.com/glamour/videos/10155637551490479/

REFLECT – A CONVERSATION WITH HERSELF

Shift #1 – The first thing Reese did was recognize the Narrative at work. The phrase she was asked to say - *what do we do now?* - did not reflect what she knew deep down. Awareness was the first step, and then she started to have conversations with others.

Shift #2 – Taking the advice of her strong mother - *if you want something done honey, do it yourself* - Reese turned to <u>herself</u> and asked, "So, what do we do now?"

Shift #3 – When launching a studio focused on the stories of women, she was repeatedly told, "There is not a market for movies about female-driven stories" – another example of the Narrative at work. Reese chose not to believe that and did a rewrite of her own.

CHOOSE –

WHAT REESE CHOSE TO DO AT THE INTERSECTION

Reese Witherspoon launched a film production studio in 2012. The studio is dedicated to female-driven material; it's all about sharing the stories of strong, powerful women. As you heard in the video, that decision resulted in half a billion dollars in sales worldwide and Academy Award nominations. Reese continues her quest, along with others in entertainment, to support women and dismantle the Narrative through the Time's Up initiative launched January 1, 2018. Another group, 50/50by2020, is pushing entertainment organizations and companies to agree to reach gender parity in their leadership tiers within two years. Be inspired – times are changing.

Key Message: Lead the change you want to see.

Many of the true story video links included in this book follow the same thought process outlined above. A sister paused long enough to recognize the Narrative for what it was. They spent time reflecting on how they could change it. Most importantly, they made a powerful choice to take action. Change our words, change our world.

#SpottheNarrative   #RewritetheNarrative

A Message From Kim

YourLionInside.com Video 7

I would love to hear your story too - Kim@
KimberlyFaith.com

Kimberly
FAITH

HARNESSING·OUR·POWER·EVERYDAY

About the Author

Kimberly Faith has had the privilege to train, coach and inspire over 24,000 leaders from 33 countries spanning 21 industries, from companies such as Amazon, American Airlines, BMW, Capgemini, DELL, GE, HCA, Nielsen and Target. In addition to working on domestic licensing deals with Warner Brothers and Disney, she has led workshops in Canada, Dubai, France, Italy and Singapore.

Influenced early in her career by the discipline of systems thinking, Kim's work in the field was included in Dr. Peter Senge's *The Fifth Discipline Fieldbook*. Her executive coaching experience led to the development of BreakthruBranding. com, an online course that inspires professionals to jump into the driver's seat of their career. Kim has been featured in Women's Entrepreneurship, Ladies Who Launch, *The Wall*

Street Journal and *Women's World*. She co-authored her first book, *Unleash Your BS (Best Self)*, in 2015.

Your Lion Inside is the first of two books. The second, *The Miss Priss Story: The Miracle of Change*, is co-authored with her mentor and friend, Linda Dolny, to be released in 2018.

"The essence of this book is to magnify H.O.P.E. - Harnessing Our Power Everyday – and to ignite what has been dormant within. I am on a quest to inspire people - and enterprises - to find where they soulfully belong and make their unique contribution to the matrix of life. May we encourage those above us, motivate those beside us and leave a legacy of empowerment for our daughters and all of those coming after us."

@KimberlyFaith1   Kim@KimberlyFaith.com

FAITH

I have been remiss in mentioning my best friend, Faith. She has been with me since birth *(Kimberly Faith Johnson),* but I never paid her much attention. She was like that annoying big sister who thinks she knows it all. I wanted no part of her in my early years. I had new paths to forge and my own blueprint for this journey called life.

At 23, I told her we would not be friends any more. I erased her name from my memory once I started a family of my own (Kim Madden). It made her sad. Faith waited. Patiently. She knew I would come around. Eventually.

It takes some of us longer than others.

A few esoteric two by fours later, at 39, life as I unknowingly designed it fell apart. Everything I once knew and believed in was shattered. During those dark days, Faith would visit me. Often. Sometimes, she would yell to get my attention. Other times, she would reason with me. Gently, and sometimes not so much, reminding me of who I was meant to be.

We would visit in quiet places, with few others around. Sadly, I would talk to her only when I had to. When no one else would take my calls.

I was not a good friend to her in those days.

Around 42, I started to remember. I learned how to tap into my power within, slowly at first. Then with gusto! My confidence increased and boy, did she have fun watching me grow into the fullness of who I was.

It had been there the entire time. My focus on other things had blinded me to the Truth.

By 45, Faith and I were best friends again. I was ready to share her with the world. Some ask what I learned from her along the way.

Faith led me back to my divine creator showing me it was my bedrock all along.

Faith taught me to believe in others – their goodness, their dharma, their humanity.

Most importantly, Faith taught me to believe in myself. My power, my strength, my divine ability to make a difference.

The good news? Now she only has to whisper when I need encouragement. "Don't forget your LION inside," she beckons.

And as simple as that, I remember. It is my deepest H.O.P.E. you will too.

Notes

BREAKING FREE

Gas was over $4.00 gallon Leigh A. Caldwell, "Face the Facts: A Fact Check on Gas Prices," CBC News, March 21, 2012, https://www.cbsnews.com/news/face-the-facts-a-fact-check-on-gas-prices/.

Structures drive behavior Peter M. Senge, *The Fifth Discipline: The Art and Practice of the Learning Organization*, Rev. and updated (New York: Doubleday/Currency, 2006). pg 40 a variation of structures influence behavior

TIME IS AN ILLUSION

19th amendment http://susanbanthonyhouse.org/her-story/suffrage-movement.php

Achievements of Susan B. Anthony "Susan B. Anthony House : Her Story." Susan B. Anthony House, http://susanbanthonyhouse.org/her-story/biography.php.

A certain book called out to me Cope, Stephen. In *The Great Work of Your Life: A Guide for the Journey to Your True Calling*, 1st ed. New York: Bantam Books, 2012.

Susan B. Anthony did have a message that day Anirudh. "10 MAJOR ACCOMPLISHMENTS OF SUSAN B ANTHONY." Learnodo Newtonic, October 5, 2015. https://learnodo-newtonic.com/susan-b-anthony-accomplishments.

No great character in American has been more ill-served Cope, Stephen. In *The Great Work of Your Life: A Guide for the Journey to Your True Calling*, 1st ed. New York: Bantam Books, 2012. pg 91

Good enough public speaker Cope, Stephen. In *The Great Work of Your Life: A Guide for the Journey to Your True Calling*, 1st ed. New York: Bantam Books, 2012. pg 97

Elizabeth Cady Stanton "Stanton/Anthony Friendship | The Susan B. Anthony Center," University of Rochester, n.d., http://www.rochester.edu/sba/suffrage-history/stantonanthony-friendship/.

Clarina Howard Nichols, Such will be your history Cope, Stephen. In *The Great Work of Your Life: A Guide for the Journey to Your True Calling*, 1st ed. New York: Bantam Books, 2012. pg 97-98

Mobilize women to act for themselves Cope, Stephen. In *The Great Work of Your Life: A Guide for the Journey to Your True Calling*, 1st ed. New York: Bantam Books, 2012. pg 98

International Women's Day "About International Women's Day." International Women's Day, http://www.internationalwomensday.com/About

#MeToo http://www.independent.co.uk/news/world/women-me-too-hashtag-twitter-sexual-harassment-stories-trending-him-though-men-responsibility-a8004806.html

Your conscious mind is telling you one story Paul Selig Trilogy by Paul Selig, (Penguin Publishing Group, 2016) Paul Selig, The Book of Knowing and Worth: A Channeled Text (Penguin, 2013).Paul Selig, The Book of Truth: The Mastery Trilogy: (Penguin, 2017).

THE GLASS CEILING IS ALSO A MIRROR

Pot roast parable I have shared this story for over twenty years. I have never been able to find the origin of the story but it is used routinely. Madora Kibbe, "The Pot Roast Principle," Psychology Today, February 8, 2014, https://www.psychologytoday.com/blog/thinking-makes-it-so/201402/the-pot-roast-principle.

Sheryl Sandberg: Lean In https://leanin.org/book/ Sheryl Sandberg, *Lean in: Women, Work, and the Will to Lead*, First edition (New York: Alfred A. Knopf, 2013).

Pushback began https://thestoryexchange.org/lean-sparks-push/ Julie Weeks, "Lean In Sparks Push Back," The Story Exchange, April 4, 2013, https://thestoryexchange.org/lean-sparks-push/.

Women must endure inaccurate perceptions   Caryl Rivers and Rosalind C. Barnett, "8 Big Problems for Women in the Workplace," Chicago Tribune, May 18, 2016, http://www.chicagotribune.com/news/opinion/commentary/ct-women-pay-gap-   workplace-equality-perspec-0519-jm-20160518-story.html.

The Narrative *derived from the idea that the system has a life of its own* Peter M. Senge, *The Fifth Discipline: The Art and Practice of the Learning Organization*, Rev. and updated (New York: Doubleday /Currency, 2006). pg. 89 (systems seem to have a mind of their own).   And Art Kleiner et al., The Fifth Discipline Fieldbook: Strategies for Building a Learning Organization (Hodder & Stoughton, 2011).

Victimhood: A mean girl of our mindset Donella Meadows, *Thinking in Systems: A Primer* (Chelsea Green Publishing, 2008). pg 157 "There is a systematic tendency on the part of human beings to avoid accountability for their own decisions."

Silicon Valley Wall Street Journal article on August 18, 2017 titled Gender Bias Runs Deep in Technology by Li Yuan Li Yuan, "Gender Bias Runs Deep in Technology," *Wall Street Journal*, August 18, 2017.

Female CEO's   "The 2017 Fortune 500 List Has More Women CEOs Than Ever Before," Fortune, http://fortune.com/2017/06/07/fortune-women-ceos/.

Firsts   "TIME Firsts: Women Leaders Who Are Changing the World," Time, http://time.com/collection/firsts/.

Person of the Year   Stephanie Zacharek, Eliana Dockterman, Haley Sweetland Edwards, "TIME Person of the Year 2017: The Silence Breakers," Time, http://time.com/time-person-of-the-year-2017-silence-breakers/.

You are the hero you seek – inspired by Paul Selig book The Book of Knowing & Truth pg 77 and The Fifth Discipline pg 21 reference to "true proactiveness"

Day by day, decision by decision Day by day, decision by decision Linda Dolny & Kimberly Faith, Day by day, decision by decision – The Miss Priss Story (2018) Original phrase by Linda Dolny.

Workplace Report   "Getting to Gender Equality Starts with Realizing How Far We Have to Go," Women in the Workplace Study, accessed December 23, 2017, https://womenintheworkplace.com/.

Article by Sheryl Sandberg in WSJ Sept 27, 2016 titled Women are Leaning in but They Face Pushback Sheryl Sandberg, "Sheryl Sandberg: Women Are Leaning In—but They Face Pushback," *Wall Street Journal,* September 27, 2016, http://www.wsj.com/articles/sheryl-sandberg-women-are-leaning-inbut- they.face-pushback-1474963980.

Countries   right   to   vote   http://www.ournellie.com/timeline-womens-suffrage-granted-country/

Shifting the Burden http://www.systems-thinking.org/theWay/ssb/sb.htm "Shifting the Burden," Systems Thinking, http://www.systems-thinking.org/theWay/ssb/sb.htm. Donella Meadows, *Thinking in Systems: A Primer* (Chelsea Green Publishing, 2008). pg 131

Celebrate 100th anniversary – books that influenced my perception of Susan B. Anthony

Elizabeth Cady Stanton & Susan B. Anthony: A friendship that changed the world by Penny Colman Penny Colman, *Elizabeth Cady Stanton and Susan B. Anthony: A Friendship That Changed the World* (Henry Holt and Company (BYR), 2013).

The World Split Open by Ruth Rosen Ruth Rosen, *The World Split Open: How the Modern Women's Movement Changed America*, Penguin Books (New York: Penguin Books, 2006).

Women's March https://www.womensmarch.com/.

International Women's Day https://www.internationalwomens-day.com/

Fearless Girl and Charging Bull James Barron, "Wounded by 'Fearless Girl,' Creator of 'Charging Bull' Wants Her to Move," *The New York Times,* April 12, 2017, https://www.nytimes.com/2017/04/12/nyregion/charging-bull-sculpture-wall-street-fearless-girl.html.

Breaking the Glass Ceiling Starts with Changing Workplace Culture Lydia Belanger, "Breaking the Glass Ceiling Starts With Changing Workplace Culture," Entrepreneur, April 7, 2017, https://www.entrepreneur.com/article/292514.

Equal Pay Day http://www.equalpaytoday.org/equal-pay-day-2017/

Can't stay in hotel alone and children assets of husband
Elizabeth Cady Stanton & Susan B. Anthony: A friendship that changed the world by Penny Colman pg 92 & 93 Penny Colman, *Elizabeth Cady Stanton and Susan B. Anthony: A Friendship That Changed the –World* (Henry Holt and Company (BYR), 2013).

Can't speak in public Elizabeth Cady Stanton & Susan B. Anthony: A friendship that changed the world by Penny Colman pg 22 Penny Colman, *Elizabeth Cady Stanton and Susan B. Anthony: A Friendship That Changed the World* (Henry Holt and Company (BYR), 2013).

When we look through both lenses Peter M. Senge, *The Fifth Discipline: The Art and Practice of the Learning Organization*, Rev. and updated (New York: Doubleday/Currency, 2006). pg 101 Balancing feedback loop

Self-fulfilling   phrophecy   "The   Self-Fulfilling Prophecy",University Discoveries, http://university-discoveries.com/the-self-fulfilling-prophecy.

Self-fulfilling phrophecy teacher example Lee Jussim, "Teacher Expectations: Self-Fulfilling Prophecies, Perceptual Biases, and Accuracy.," *Journal of Personality and Social Psychology* 57, no. 3 (1989): 469–80, https://doi.org/10.1037/0022-3514.57.3.469.

We have all felt the effect Miles Kohrman and Miles Kohrman, "8 Subconscious Mistakes Our Brains Make Every Day–And How To Avoid Them," Fast Company, October 15, 2013, https://www.fastcompany.com/3019903/8-subconscious-mistakes-our-brains-make-every-day-and-how-to-avoid-them.

Also influenced by the following books –

Joe Dispenza, *Breaking the Habit of Being Yourself: How to Lose Your Mind and Create a New One* (Hay House, Inc, 2012).

Daniel Kahneman, *Thinking, Fast and Slow* (Farrar, Straus and Giroux, 2011).

Dr. Matthew Price http://www.linkedin.com/in/mattprice0926

Sentiment analysis   Gigi DeVault, "Don't Get All Sentimental on Us," The Balance, April 13, 2017, https://www.thebalance.com/what-is-sentiment-analysis-2296941.

Centiment Micah Brown, "Micah Brown Articles," Centiment Blog, accessed December 23, 2017, https://centiment.io/beta/blog/author/micah-brown-ceo/. *All screenshots of data were created utilizing the software from Centiment at various times throughout 2017.

Micah Brown   *Centiment Demo Day,* 2017, https://vimeo.com/223705717.

Bandwagon effect Linda Bloom and Charlie Bloom, "The Bandwagon Effect," Psychology Today, August 11, 2017, https://www.psychologytoday.com/blog/stronger-the-broken-places/201708/the-bandwagon-effect.

Availability Heuristic   "Availability Heuristic," *iResearch-Net* , http://psychology.iresearchnet.com/social-psychology/social- cognition/availability-heuristic/.

Anchoring "The Effects of Anchoring Bias on Human Behavior," SAGU, May 23, 2016, https://www.sagu.edu/thoughthub/the affects-of-anchoring-bias-on-human-behavior.

Parable of the boiled frog Peter M. Senge, *The Fifth Discipline: The Art and Practice of the Learning Organization,* Rev. and updated (New York: Doubleday/Currency, 2006). Pg 22

Downplay the Difference study by Ashley E. Martin and katherine W. Phillips titled What Blindness to gender differences helps women see and do Ashley E. Martin and Katherine W. Phillips, "What 'blindness' to Gender Differences Helps Women See and Do: Implications for Confidence, Agency, and Action in Male Dominated Environments," *Organizational Behavior and Human Decision Processes* 142 (September 2017): 28–44, https://doi.org/10.1016/j.obhdp.2017.07.004.

Power and Gender Identification Study by Andrea C. Vial and James L. Napier titled High Power Mindsets reduce gender identification Andrea C. Vial and Jaime L. Napier, "High Power Mindsets Reduce Gender Identification and Benevolent Sexism among Women (But Not Men)," *Journal of Experimental Social Psychology* 68 (January 2017): 162–70, https://doi.org/10.1016/j.jesp.2016.06.012.

Hollywood Isn't Helping – study was by Souha R. Ezzdeen titled The Portrayal of professional and managerial women in North American Films Souha R. Ezzedeen, "The Portrayal of Professional and Managerial Women in North American Films," *Organizational Dynamics* 42, no. 4 (October 2013): 248–56, https://doi.org/10.1016/j.orgdyn.2013.07.002.

Glass Ceiling phrase "The Glass Ceiling," *The Economist*, May 5, 2009, http://www.economist.com/node/13604240.

Times   Up https://www.nytimes.com/2018/01/01/movies/times-up-hollywood-women-sexual-harassment.html

Unintended consequences Donella Meadows, *Thinking in Systems: A Primer* (Chelsea Green Publishing, 2008). pg 111 regarding non- linear thinking

Hidden Figures movie Margot Lee Shetterly, *Hidden Figures: The American Dream and the Untold Story of the Black Women Mathematicians Who Helped Win the Space Race* (HarperCollins, 2016).

Bamboo ceiling Jane Hyun, Breaking the Bamboo Ceiling: Career Strategies for Asians (Harper Collins, 2009).

THE DNA OF THOUGHT

DNA insight Donella Meadows, *Thinking in Systems: A Primer* (Chelsea Green Publishing, 2008). pg 159

Origin of DNA Ancestry Deborah A. Bolnick et al., "The Science and Business of Genetic Ancestry Testing," *Science* 318, no. 5849 (October 19, 2007): 399–400, https://doi.org/10.1126/science.1150098.

Origin of DNA health kits Gina Kolata, "With a Simple DNA Test, Family Histories Are Rewritten," *The New York Times*, August 28, 2017, sec. Science, https://www.nytimes.com/2017/08/28/science/dna-tests-ancestry.html

DNA   Forensics https://www.justice.gov/archives/ag/advancing-justice-through-dna-technology- using-dna-solve-crimes

Loss of 100 pounds Libby Birk, "Real Tips From Women Who Have Lost 30 Pounds Or More," Womanista, October 7, 2016, http://womanista.com/wellness/2016/10/07/real-tips-from-women-who-have-lost-30-pounds-or- more/.

THE TOOLKIT

Mental models Peter M. Senge, *The Fifth Discipline: The Art and Practice of the Learning Organization*, Rev. and updated (New York: Doubleday/Currency, 2006) Chapter 10 starting pg 174. And Donella Meadows, *Thinking in Systems: A Primer* (Chelsea Green Publishing, 2008). pg 86 and 172-175

Kodak "What Killed Kodak?," *Philip Sayer* (blog), October 16, 2012, https://philsayer.net/2012/10/16/what-killed-kodak/.

Sony story Gillian Tett, *The Silo Effect: The Peril of Expertise and the Promise of Breaking Down Barriers* (Simon and Schuster, 2015).

It has been called the biggest miss in the board room Celena Chong, "Blockbuster's CEO Once Passed up a Chance to Buy Netflix for Only $50 Million," Business Insider, July 17, 2015, http://www.businessinsider.com/blockbuster-ceo-passed-up-chance-to-   buy-netflix-for-50-million-2015-7.

As we enter an age http://fortune.com/2017/09/13/gm-cruise-self-driving-driverless-autonomous-cars/ ; http://fortune.com/2017/12/26/4-technology-trends-2018/   ;   https://www.pcmag.com/article/351486/blockchain-the-invisible-technology-thats-changing-the-wor

The dance of change – subtitle inspired by The Fifth Discipline Fieldbook My community was spotlighted on page 502-504 I was very involved with the writing and documentation of the story. Peter M. Senge, *The Fifth Discipline: The Art and Practice of the Learning Organization*, Rev. and updated (New York: Doubleday/Currency, 2006). Also inspired by Thinking in Systems book by Donella Meadows pg 170 Donella Meadows, *Thinking in Systems: A Primer* (Chelsea Green Publishing, 2008).

Pause, reflect, choose Peter M. Senge, *The Fifth Discipline: The Art and Practice of the Learning Organization*, Rev. and updated (New York: Doubleday/Currency, 2006). pg. 195 and pg 360 variation based on leaps of abstraction

The pivot zone Dan Baker Ph.D and Cameron Stauth, *What Happy People Know: How the New Science of Happiness Can Change Your Life for the Better*, 1 edition (St. Martin's Griffin, 2004). Pg 135

MEET THE SISTERHOOD

Tin cans clanking, loud and unnecessary Paul Selig, *The Book of Mastery* (Penguin Publishing Group, 2016). Pg 39

Fear has fangs Dan Baker Ph.D and Cameron Stauth, *What Happy People Know: How the New Science of Happiness Can Change Your Life for the Better*, 1 edition (St. Martin's Griffin, 2004). Pg 132

Happen like a light switch Donella Meadows, *Thinking in Systems: A Primer* (Chelsea Green Publishing, 2008). pg 163-164

THE KARI STORY

Energy – I first learned about the concept of energy from Kelli Fenters, healer and angel intuitive. You can find her at IeAmKelli.com Ie AM Kelli: Holistic Wellness, Self-Discovery Mentor, Angel Guidance, http://www.ieamkelli.com/.

Done is better than perfect phrase – a phrase I had said for many years as you will see in the story below. When I read Lean In and saw that it resonated with Sheryl Sandberg, I knew they were sisters too

> *I remember being a full-time working mom and receiving subtle criticism from a well-meaning stay-at-home mom. The comment reinforced my desire to be the perfect employee, the perfect citizen, the perfect mother. My daughter was five years old when I was asked to bring a special snack to the Easter party - in the days before Pinterest (gasp!). I remember tearing a delightful snack idea out of a parenting magazine. For five hours I slaved away, creating darling little caramel-covered egg noodles shaped to look like bird nests.*

> *I clumsily created homemade chocolate eggs decorated to the nines to lovingly place into the nests. I carefully packed them all and took them to the party.*

> *The stay-at-home mom who had "inspired" me to discover my inner Betty Crocker marveled at my masterpiece. At the end of the party, I was cleaning up and to my chagrin, NOT ONE OF THE MASTERPIECES WAS EATEN! The children thought they looked funny – how dare they? I watched hours of my life go into the trash. At that moment, I realized that "done is better*

than perfect." For the next party, I purchased a box of crackers. Done.

Songs, Movies, Books, & True Stories

India Arie, *Strength Courage & Wisdom*, Audio CD (Universal Import, 2002).

Franklin Aretha, *A Rose Is Still a Rose*, Audio CD (Arista, 1998).

Janelle Monáe, *Q.U.E.E.N.*, 2013.

Aguilera Christina, *Beautiful*, Audio CD (Bmg Int'l, 2003).

Born This Way, Audio CD (Interscope Records, 2011). Lady Gaga, *Born This Way*, Audio CD (Interscope Records, 2011).

Brene Brown, *The Gifts of Imperfection: Let Go of Who You Think You're Supposed to Be and Embrace Who You Are* (Hazelden Publishing, 2010).

Ron Clements and John Musker, *Moana*, Animation, Adventure, 2016.

Cheryl Strayed, *Wild: From Lost to Found on the Pacific Crest Trail* (Knopf Doubleday Publishing Group, 2012).

Great Big Story, *Untangling the Roots of Dominican Hair*, accessed December 24, 2017, https://www.youtube.com/watch?v=XwtnFGB9c_c.

The Stay At Home Chef, *Why My Gray Hairs Make Me Happy*, 2016 https://www.youtube.com/watch?v=aFk9L3nhS0Q&feat re=youtu.be.

"Mel Robbins -Outsmart Your Brain," Goalcast, July 24, 2017, https://www.goalcast.com/2017/07/24/mel-robbins-felt-like-a-complete-failure/.

Kidada Jones, School of Awake https://youtu.be/16f_x4Qhycw OWN, SuperSoul Short: Kidada Jones, School of Awake | SuperSoul Sunday | Oprah Winfrey Network, 2017, https://www.youtube.com/watch?v=16f_x4Qhycw&feature=youtu.be.

*I asked for suggestions from many colleagues when it came to gathering songs, books, movies and true stories to inspire. There are many more examples to be added in the future. This list is simply to get you started and are recommendations only. KF Enterprises, Inc., or Kimberly Faith, has no liability for content in third party materials or links.

THE RANEE STORY

Songs, Movies, Books, & True Stories

Kristin Chenoweth & Idina Menzel, *Defying Gravity*, Audio CD (Verve, 2003). Meghan Trainor, *NO*, Audio CD (Epic, 2016).

Golden Moments, Audio CD (Hidden Beach Records, 2015).

Lesley Gore, *You Don't Own Me*, Audio CD (Hip-O Records, 1963).

David Frankel, *The Devil Wears Prada*,Drama, 2006, http://www.imdb.com/title/tt0458352/. Mike Newell

Mona Lisa Smile, Drama, 2003, http://www.imdb.com/title/tt0304415/.

Martin Ritt, *Norma Rae*, Drama, 1979, http://www.imdb.com/title/tt0079638/.

Melinda Gates Makes a Difference CBS Sunday Morning, *Q&A: Melinda Gates*, 2017, https://www.youtube.com/watch?v=yu45Ct- dzoM.

The Art of Childbirth Michelle Hartney is a true "Instigator," using her probing art to shine a light on the increasing dangers of childbirth in the United States. This is the second part of the"Instigators" series, which profiles people fighting for change in women's health.

"I Don't Need Her Permission": Art as a Weapon for Women, 2015, http://www.greatbigstory.com/stories/instigators-michelle-hartney-s-quest-to-give-women-a- choice.

Designing for Inclusivity 99U, *Liz Jackson: Designing for Inclusivity*, 2017, http://99u.com/videos/55965/liz-jackson- designing-for-inclusivity.

THE GABRIELLA STORY

Songs, Movies, Books, & True Stories

Beyoncé feat. Kendrick Lamar, *Freedom*, Audio CD ("Freedom" by Beyonce, 2016).

Demi Lovato, *Confident*, Audio CD (Hollywood Records, 2015).

Kelly Clarkson, *Stronger*, Audio CD (RCA Records Label, 2011).

Whitney Houston, *Greatest Love Of All*, Audio CD (Arista, 1985).

Rita Ora, *Grateful*, Audio CD (RELATIVITY MUSIC 2, 2014).

Steven Soderbergh, *Erin Brockovich*, Biography, Drama, 2000, http://www.imdb.com/title/tt0195685/.

Sanjay Leela Bhansali, *Black*, Drama, 2005, http://www.imdb.com/title/tt0375611/.

Nigeria's First Female Mechanic Nigeria's First Female Car Mechanic Is Changing the World (Great Big Story, 2016), http://www.greatbigstory.com/stories/meet-nigeria-s-first-female-car-mechanic.

A Woman Who Dared to Drive Manal al-Sharif, *A Saudi Woman Who Dared to Drive*, 2013, https://www.ted.com/talks/manal_al_sharif_a_saudi_woman_who_dared_to_drive.

A One Woman's Fight Against Hate Atika Shubert and Nadine Schmidt, "The Septuagenarian Fighting Hate with a Spray Can," CNN, December 17, 2016, http://edition.cnn.com/2016/12/17/europe/irmela-schramm-fights-berlin-street-art-racism/index.html.

THE DARSHA STORY

Songs, Movies, Books, & True Stories

Christina Aguilera, *Fighter*, Audio CD (Bmg/Arista, 2003).

Nina Simone, *Feeling Good: The Very Best Of*, Audio CD (Universal I.S., 2004).

Taylor Swift, *Shake It Off*, Audio CD (Big Machine Records, LLC, 2014).

Katy Perry, *Roar*, Audio CD (Universal Import, 2013).

The Black Eyed Peas, *Own It*, Audio CD (Interscope, 2010).

Theodore Melfi, *Hidden Figures*, Biography, Drama, History, 2017, http://www.imdb.com/title/tt4846340/.

Tate Taylor, *The Help*, Drama, 2011, http://www.imdb.com/title/tt1454029/.

Trina Paulus, *Hope for the Flowers* (LLC, 2014). https://www.amazon.com/gp/product/B00LLOQ16Q?tag=kfo010e-

Great Big Story, *Creating Community With Spain's All-Female Cricket Team*, 2017, https://www.greatbigstory.com/stories/creating-community-with-spain-s-all-female-cricket-team.

Great Big Story, *Fitness Goals: Bodybuilding at 80*, 2017, https://www.greatbigstory.com/stories/fitness-goals-bodybuilding-at-80-years-old.

"The Power to Live and Forgive.," September 26, 2017, https://www.facebook.com/BuzzFeed/videos/10156791799070329/.

THE AVALENE STORY

Songs, Movies, Books, & True Stories

Little Mix, *Salute*, Audio CD (Sony Legacy, 2014).

Diana Ross, *I'm Coming Out*, Audio CD (Motown, 1980).

Whitney Houston, *I'm Every Woman*, Audio CD (Arista, 1993).

Jennifer Hudson & Jennifer Nettles, *You Will*, Audio CD (RCA Records Label, 2015).

Mark Waters, *Mean Girls*, Comedy, 2004, http://www.imdb.com/title/tt0377092/.

Sue Monk Kidd, *The Secret Life of Bees*, 1st edition (New York: Penguin Books, 2003).

Penny Marshall, A League of Their Own, Family, 1992, http://www.imdb.com/title/tt0104694/. Ridley Scott, G.I. Jane, Action, Drama, War, 1997, http://www.imdb.com/title/tt0119173/.

All Female Sushi House Great Big Story, *Inside Japan's Only All-Female Sushi House*, 2017, https://www.greatbigstory.com/stories/all-female-sushi-house.

Upstanders A Racists Rehabilitation "Upstanders: A Racist's Rehabilitation," Starbucks Newsroom, October 18, 2017, https://news.starbucks.com/news/upstanders-a-racists-rehabilitation.

Instigators the Midwife of La Cienega Boulevard Great Big Story, *Instigators: The Midwife of La Cienega Boulevard*, 2015, https://www.greatbigstory.com/stories/instigators-the-midwife-of-la-cienega-boulevard.

THE JALILA STORY

Busyness becomes a major blindspot Donella Meadows, *Thinking in Systems: A Primer* (Chelsea Green Publishing, 2008). pg 89 events level of thinking and Peter M. Senge, *The Fifth Discipline: The Art and Practice of the Learning Organization*, Rev. and updated (New York: Doubleday/ Currency, 2006). Pg 52

Own and articulate your value – Mika Brzezinski, *Knowing Your Value: Women, Money, and Getting What You're Worth*, Reprint edition (Hachette Books, 201

Destiny's Child, *Independent Women Pt. I*, Audio CD (Columbia, 2003).

Aretha Franklin, *Respect*, Audio CD (Flashback - Rhino, 1997).

Mary J. Blige, *Just Fine* (Geffen, 2007).

Ani DiFranco, *Not a Pretty Girl*, Audio CD (RIGHTEOUS BABE RECORDS, 2017).

Robert Luketic, *Legally Blonde*, Comedy, Romance, 2001, http://www.imdb.com/title/tt0250494/.

Malala Yousafzai and Christina Lamb, *I Am Malala: The Girl Who Stood Up for Education and Was Shot by the Taliban*, 1st edition (New York: Little, Brown and Company, 2013).

Great Big Story, *High Fashion's Hijab Queen*, 2017, https://www.greatbig-story.com/stories/high-fashion-s-hijab-queen.

Great Big Story, *Claressa: Fighting to Stay on Top*, 2016, https://www.greatbigstory.com/stories/claressa#.

THE NIKKI STORY

Variation of Margaret Mead famous quote: Never Doubt That a Small Group of Thoughtful, Committed Citizens Can Change the World; Indeed, It's the Only Thing That Ever Has

Kelly Clarkson, Chloe x Halle, Missy Elliott, Kelly Rowland & Zendaya, Janelle Monáe, Lea Michele, Jadagrace, *Michelle Obama All-Star Girl Power Anthem - This Is for My Girls*, Audio CD (Offer Nissim Music, 2017).

Beyonce, *Run the World*, Audio CD (Parkwood Entertainment/Columbia, 2011).

Rachel Platten, *Fight Song*, Audio CD (Imports, 2015).

Natasha Bedingfield, *Unwritten*, Audio CD (Empire / Phonogenic / BMG UK & Ireland, 2004).

Alicia Keys, *Superwoman*, Audio CD (J Records, 2007).

Patty Jenkins, *Wonder Woman*, Action, Adventure, Fantasy, 2017, http://www.imdb.com/title/tt0451279/.

Steven Spielberg, *The Post*, Historical Drama, Political Thriller, 2017, http://www.imdb.com/title/tt6294822/?ref_=fn_al_tt_1

Gary Ross, *The Hunger Games*, Adventure, Sci-Fi, Thriller, 2012, http://www.imdb.com/title/tt1392170/.

Anne Fontaine, *Cocoa Before Chanel,* Biography, Drama, 2009, http://www.imdb.com/title/tt1035736/

A Field Between Great Big Story, *A Field Between | Former CIA Operative Risks Life to Promote Peace*, 2017, https://www.greatbigstory.com/stories/a-field-between-a-really-great-big-story?playall=531.

The Army of Moms Standing up to Gun Violence Great Big Story, *Taking Back the Neighborhood with an Army of Moms*, 2016, https://www.greatbigstory.com/stories/the-army-of-moms-standing-up-to-gun-violence.

A Café Run by Heroes Great Big Story, *A Cafe Run by Heroes*, 2016, https://www.greatbigstory.com/stories/a-cafe-run-by-heroes.

HOW THE SISTERHOOD COMES TO LIFE

An inspiration guide – my attempt to reduce complexity based on systems principle Peter M. Senge, *The Fifth Discipline: The Art and Practice of the Learning Organization*, Rev. and updated (New York: Doubleday/Currency, 2006). pg 281-284

Hay House publishing conference https://youtu.be/bJka9GI39iE Kimberly Faith, *Hay House Inspirational Testimonial Video for SWP Conference 2016*, September 10, 2016, https://www.youtube.com/watch?v=bJka9GI39iE&feature=youtu.be.

Power of intention Wayne W. Dyer, *The Power of Intention* (Hay House, Inc, 2010).

In the eyes of a 101 year old - mantra Wall Street Journal article by Elizabeth Berstein May 9, 2017 titled Say It Again, A Mantra Really Works

BEFORE I KNEW THE SISTERHOOD

I will be Vice President Eve Gumpel, "Working With My Mom," Entrepreneur, May 9, 2008, https://www.entrepreneur.com/article/218041.

Boldly took the leap Kim Madden and Heather Madden, "President/ Sassy Empress & 8 Yrs. Old, VP of Ideas | Ladies Who Launch," *Ladies Who Launch* (blog), July 30, 2005, http://www.ladieswholaunch.com/magazine/presidentsassy-empress-8-yrs-old-vp-of-ideas/.

Level of growth Peter M. Senge, *The Fifth Discipline: The Art and Practice of the Learning Organization*, Rev. and updated (New York: Doubleday/Currency, 2006). pg 95 and Donella Meadows, *Thinking in Systems: A Primer* (Chelsea Green Publishing, 2008). Pg 103

Spoke to high school students DECA Event Featured in Future CEO Stars, November 2007, pg 27 http://fcs.entre-ed.org/pdf/november_year_1.pdf

Economic crash of 2008 Kimberly Amadeo, "What Caused the 2008 Financial Crisis and Could It Happen Again?," The Balance, July 1, 2017, https://www.thebalance.com/2008-financial-crisis-3305679.

Different Joanne Lipman, "That's What She Said: What Men Need to Know (and Women Need to Tell Them) About Working Together," January 2018 https://www.amazon.com/Thats-What-She-Said-Together/dp/0062437216/ref=asap_bc?ie=UTF8

Conversations https://leanin.org/together

Ruby slippers Dorothy, *The Wizard of Oz*, Adventure, 1939, Directed by: Victor Fleming and George Cukor http://www.imdb.com/title/tt0032138/.

WHEN WE ARE TEMPTED TO GIVE IN

The Feminine Mystique Betty Friedan, *The Feminine Mystique* (W. W. Norton, 2010).

The butterfly effect Jamie L. Vernon, "Understanding the Butterfly Effect," American Scientist, April 12, 2017, https://www.americanscientist.org/article/understanding-the-butterfly-effect. And Gregg Braden, *The Isaiah Effect: Decoding the Lost Science of Prayer and Prophecy* (Three Rivers Press, 2000). Pg 105

The surprising leverage Donella Meadows, *Thinking in Systems: A Primer* (Chelsea Green Publishing, 2008). Pg 145

The heartbreaking USA Gymnastics case https://www.theguardian.com/sport/2018/jan/26/larry-nassar-abuse-gymnasts-scandal-culture

Think about the significance statistics http://fortune.com/2017/10/17/me-too-hashtag-sexual-harassment-at-work-stats/ and http://www.stopdv.org/index.php/statistics/ and https://www.respect.gov.au/wp-content/uploads/2016/06/conversation_guide.pdf Impressive guide about respect.

In many ways we have changed reality https://blog.dol.gov/2017/03/01/12-stats-about-working-women

We boldly step out https://www.cnn.com/2018/01/26/entertainment/octavia-spencer-jessica-chastain-pay/index.html

Stop accepting the unacceptable Time Magazine 2017 Person of the Year The Silence Breakers Editor in Chief. Stephanie Zacharek, Eliana Dockterman, Haley Sweetland Edwards, "TIME Person of the Year 2017: The Silence Breakers," Time, http://time.com/time-person-of-the-year-2017-silence-breakers/.

Banging my head against his-story phrase – inspired by Ellen Pao's brave story Ellen Pao, *Reset: My Fight for Inclusion and Lasting Change* (Random House Publishing Group, 2017).

Blame serves no one – the answers we seek are not outside of ourselves Peter M. Senge, *The Fifth Discipline: The Art and Practice of the Learning Organization*, Rev. and updated (New York: Doubleday/Currency, 2006). pg 19 variation of the enemy is out there

Love Warrior for humanity – inspired by Glennon Doyle, *Love Warrior: A Memoir* (Hachette UK, 2016).

Golden Age Kaia Ra, *The Sophia Code: A Living Transmission from the Sophia Dragon Tribe* (CreateSpace Independent Publishing Platform, 2016). Pg. 45

Fear or love Marianne Williamson, *Tears to Triumph: The Spiritual Journey from Suffering to Enlightenment* (HarperCollins, 2016). pg 14, 76, 78, and 111

Alchemy of thought Inspired by Paulo Coelho, *The Alchemist* (HarperCollins, 2006).

CONCLUSION

Is the illusion Paul Selig, *I Am the Word: A Guide to the Consciousness of Man's Self in a Transitioning Time* (Penguin, 2010). Pg 35

Life waiting for you (shared vision) as explained through her-story Peter M. Senge, *The Fifth Discipline: The Art and Practice of the Learning Organization*, Rev. and updated (New York: Doubleday/Currency, 2006). Chapter 11 starting on page 205

A MESSAGE TO MY SWEET SISTERS

Warning to my sisters – Jerold A. Sinnamon, "Finding the Right Leverage Point," The Systems Thinker, February 20, 2016, https://thesystemsthinker.com/finding-the-right-leverage-point/.

WAYS TO SPOT (AND REWRITE) THE NARRATIVE

Self-full phrase and reference to never bleach a red flag – Carol Mann http://yourcosmiccafe.com/

https://www.vanityfair.com/news/2015/03/mellody-hobson-ariel-investments-fighting-stereotype

https://www.vanityfair.com/news/2015/03/mellody-hobson-ariel-investments-fighting-stereotype

Acknowledgements

My beloved Peter – In the heart space that is you, you gave me a safe place to blossom. I will forever be grateful. Your legacy lives on. You are dearly loved. I am your girl, now and forever.

Heather – You are the light of my life. You have inspired me in so many ways. Thank you for leading me to the best version of myself.

Kat Walsh – Kindred spirit. Shared passion. A vision for a better world for our daughters. What an amazing editor and partner you have been! Thank you for being fully present on this journey with me and the Sisterhood. Your spark and light is infused into the essence of the book.

Mom – Thank you for teaching me how to be strong. Know that our journey will make a difference in the lives of many.

Dad – Sometimes our greatest lessons come from the toughest intersections. You taught me to be a fighter and for that I am grateful.

Amy & Paul – A brother is a special gift. When he brings a fabulous sister-in-law into the picture, it is an added bonus. Amy, thank you for your ongoing encouragement in bringing this dream to life. Together we are creating a better world for Pi & Sullie.

Linda Dolny – You are a living example of how one person can change the world one life at a time. Thank you for your wisdom and love.

Rose – In February 2018 we will celebrate your 102nd birthday. I know you have wondered many times why you are still here. Maybe it was to be a part of the magic of this book. Your story lives on.

To all the "sisters" who allowed me to use their story as inspiration in this book – You are such an important part of *her-story*. Thank you for the privilege to be a part of your journey. Your willingness to be included in this book will make a difference to many.

Kelli Fenters – I don't know where I would be if God had not brought you into my life in 2009. Good thing the divine knew I needed extra help. www.ieamKelli.com

Liz Wiltsie – Thank you for sharing the Sassytails dream - our passion lives on.

BB – Every major step in my life, you have been there. Words will never be big enough to thank you.

Jack Bundy – How were we to know that offering me my first 'real' job out of college set into motion a path that would lead to the creation of this book. Your vision for a better world lives on.

Jenna Powers – Our shared passion played an important role in this book. Thank you for investing time and energy in this vision. Never underestimate your power to change the world too.

Kim C. – So proud of what has unfolded as a result of our paths crossing. Powerful women changing the world for our girls.

Jeff Black – My brother from another mother, respected colleague, and dear friend. Twenty years and counting. Your support is never ending. Thank you for showing me what the life of a good man looks like. blacksheepunleashed.com

Carol Hamilton – Your love for feng shui and interpreting space was what started our journey. Thank you for seeing potential when I could not. Thrilled you and Jeff were my first co-authors with *Unleash Your BS: Best Self*. Feng Shui Coaching by Carol Hamilton

Allison Lindquist – In 2009 I stumbled into your 90Degrees Yoga studio a broken soul. The safe space nurtured me back to wholeness. A special thanks to you and your instructors for teaching me the power of the breath. <u>Devotional Awakenings - Daily Devotions</u>

Sara Kwan – An amazing and inspiring woman you are. Your energy propels many forward, including me. I will always remember to *be brave*.

Dr. Matthew Price –Thank you for sharing my vision of a better world. I have deep respect for your insights and much appreciation for your help with this book.

Reid Tracy & Cheryl Richardson – Thanks to each of you, and to Hay House, for being an important stepping stone on my journey. My eternal gratitude.

Angela, the mother at the Hay House conference – Someday I hope to be able to thank you in person for saying the right thing at the right time. Synchronicity is amazing.

Allie Orzell – You are a treasure. I knew it the first time we met. So glad you now see it too.

Cammie Mackie – My soul sister. So many things would not have unfolded if our paths had not crossed. Destiny prevailed. You are a testament to one sister making a life changing difference.

Victoria Kirby – Our adventures around the globe parallel the power of our spirit. Great chapters are still ahead. Shine your light for the world to see.

Phyllis Nolan & Despina Yeargin – Steady. Authentic. Poised. You are powerful women in my world. Thank you for your loving guidance along the way.

Phi Mu Sisters – Thank you for giving me the experience of a sisterhood in college. A special thanks to Beth Holcombe for continuing the legacy.

Tim R. – You taught me what dignity looked like through difficult times. I will always be grateful for your belief. Your investment lives on.

Amanda McTeer & Caroline Collins –   Amanda, my VA in the US and Caroline, my VA in Scotland http://ccsharedservices.com Both of you played a role in taking care of details to free up space for me to focus on the book. Thank you for your support and encouragement along the way.

Dr. Peter Senge, author of The Fifth Discipline – Grateful for your teachings. Never had a chance to see the world any other way other since I was in my early 20's when we met. Your book profoundly influenced my world and even saved my life.

Charlotte Roberts – Your work through Innovation Associates and your passion for systems thinking made a big impact on me back in the 1990's. Thank you for your leadership and wisdom in The 5th Discipline - Fieldbook Strategies.

Your Lion Inside Design Team - Thank you to Jun from the Philippines for the beautiful cover design; Emma from South Africa for the inspiring teaching artwork; Tom Fox for the black and white illustrations bringing my ideas to life; and Freda/Sonia with Freshsparks for bringing my personal message of h.o.p.e. to the world alive in vivid color. WhitneyLamb.com, your insight was invaluable.

Reading early drafts the book - Erin Hughes, Carolyn Foss, Kim Orzell, Angela Russell, LeAnne Thorfinnson, Annette Waters, and Lytia Watson: These women and countless others above read early drafts of the book to provide feedback. So grateful for your time and energy!

A special thanks to the following women for contributing ideas, thoughts, observations and questions for the book, including but not limited to - Bree Amaya, Erin Barnhart, Hao Ci Beckel, Tracy Best, Debbie Volm Bohn, Sunny Bokhari, Robyn Brands, Kathleen Buckley, Audrey Burton, Jacqueline Cahalene, Beth Camp, Robin Cantrell, Alicia Carr, Elizabeth Cary, Kim Cato, Susana Castellanos, Jessica Church, Jean Cimmena, Winnie Choe,

Allison Crosby, Andrea Daniel, Sophie Darrigues, Patricia Dolder, Jennifer Downing, Ruth Drake, Carol Dunklin, Kim Gardner, Alicia Hammersmith, Angie Harbin, Paige Hilton, Lauren Hisey, Sara Hix, Christie Hollingsworth, Michelle McNickle Driver, Mary Beth Hines, Anna Hollack, Emma Jewell Howard, Jennifer Hurst, Rhonda Huskins, Elizabeth Johnson, Wan Yi Loh, Lee Long, Jessica Johannson, Colleen Kirkpatrick, Manasi Mankame, Amanda McCauley, Linda McCoy, Alicia McLaughlin, Andy Beth Miller, Rose Miller, Jeanne Monsma, Nicole Mullins, Kate Neville, Tina Nguyen, Gina Ohansian, Belinda Olivares, Sara Orzell, Andrea Otto, Rebecca Perdue, Natalie Petruska, Nahdia Pirzada, Brittney Pullen, Tracy Robertson, Jane Rovins, Mairead Quinn, Amanda Sarratore, Sara Satterlee, Sheree Seniff, Catherine Smith, Michelle Smith, Peggy Sullivan, Sofia Svanholt, Fanaye Taye, Nancy Thomas, Kristi Timmons, Towanna Tindall, Andrea Turner, Meghan Walsh, Wendy Wilson, Janet Woodyard, Sharon Young, Karina Shatsman Zide and many, many others.

Index

Our Collective Journey

WHEN WOMEN EARNED THE RIGHT TO VOTE

1893	New Zealand
1902	Australia*
1906	Finland
1913	Norway
1915	Denmark
1917	Canada**
1918	Austria, Germany, Poland, Russia
1919	Netherlands
1920	**United States**
1921	Sweden
1928	Britain, Ireland
1931	Spain
1934	Turkey
1944	France
1945	Italy
1947	Argentina, Japan, Mexico, Pakistan
1949	China
1950	India
1954	Colombia
1957	Malaysia, Zimbabwe
1962	Algeria
1963	Iran, Morocco
1964	Libya
1967	Ecuador
1971	Switzerland
1972	Bangladesh
1974	Jordan
1976	Portugal
1988	Namibia
1990	Western Samoa
1993	Kazakhstan, Moldova
1994	South Africa
2005	Kuwait
2006	United Arab Emirates
2011	Saudi Arabia

*Aborigines, male and female, gained the right to vote in 1962.

**Canadian First Nation, male and female, did not win the vote until 1960.

https://www.usatoday.com/story/news/2018/02/05/
voting-rights-women-how-countries-stack-up/306238002/

Awareness — CURRENT MENTAL MODEL
your beliefs, mindsets

Choice — A NEW MENTAL MODEL
...this is the first step

Freedom — YOUR DESIRED FUTURE
a BIG-shift in the mental model

Mental models are the "lens" through which we see the world. The beliefs are not good or bad—they simply are. The danger is when we unconsciously operate from those beliefs. We have the power to CHOOSE!

CURRENT MENTAL MODEL	A NEW MENTAL MODEL	YOUR DESIRED FUTURE
THE KARI STORY — KARI — I expect perfection	I believe DONE is better than perfect	I AM enough
THE RANEE STORY — RANEE — I have to meet all demands	I CAN say no	Here is what I am willing to do
THE GABRIELLA STORY — GABRIELLA — I need permission/approval	I TRUST my own decisions	I can move forward *in* confidence
THE DARSHA STORY — DARSHA — I should accept what is said	I CAN pause, reflect and choose	I choose to rewrite the narrative
THE AVALENE STORY — AVALENE — I am not qualified enough	I AM the right one for the opportunity	There is enough for me AND you
THE JALILA STORY — JALILA — If I work hard enough, I will be rewarded	I can advocate and CARE for myself	I own and articulate my value
THE NIKKI STORY — NIKKI — I'm okay in the background	I AM powerful and that's okay	My power is MUCH needed in this world

Stop allowing these mindsets to stand in the way. · *Slowly allow your light to shine brighter...* · *Go forward and unleash your best self!*

VICTIMHOOD: Powerless: Defensive · Offensive: Powerful: VICTORY

For more information about
Kimberly Faith
and
Your Lion Inside
please visit:

YourLionInside.com or KimberlyFaith.com

and reach out to Kim via:

Kim@KimberlyFaith.com
www.linkedin.com/in/KimberlyFaith
Twitter: @KimberlyFaith1
www.Youtube.com/c/KimberlyFaithInspires
https://www.instagram.com/KimberlyFaithInspires/
https://www.pinterest.com/KimberlyFaithInspires/
Facebook: Kimberly Faith - Author